Ronald Fisher
120 East Cook
   St Paul Minn.

the way of a *trout*

the way of a trout

R. P. Van Gytenbeek

Color photographs by James W. Wilkie

J. B. Lippincott Company
Philadelphia and New York

U.S. Library of Congress Cataloging in Publication Data

Van Gytenbeek, R   P   birth date
  The way of a trout.

    1. Trout.   2. Trout Unlimited.   3. Nature
conservation—U.S.   I. Title.
QL638.S2V33   597′.55   72–6146
ISBN–0–397–00872–4

TO ELLIOTT
without whom there would be no
Trout Unlimited as we know it today

Foreword

There is a war going on. Battle after battle has been waged in an effort to wrest our precious resources from their delicate ecological balance. The Enemy has inflicted casualties on thousands of miles of free-flowing rivers and streams, countless wildlife, millions of fish, and man.

Fortunately the last-named can read the indicators of his well-being. Just as canaries brought by miners into the mines warned of coal-gas leaks, so trout provide the barometer of life-sustaining water. The presence of live, healthy trout is a guarantee of pure, cold water. When trout are threatened, so is man.

In recent years awareness of the shocking condition of our water resources has mushroomed. But there is also a growing frustration over the lack of effective action by industry, government, and the private sector. Democracy, by its very nature, moves slowly, and the old ways die hard. It has taken America 200 years to create the current crisis. We haven't another 200 to clean it up. What must be done, must be done now.

The question that precedes any maneuver, defensive or offensive, is always, "What can I do?" It is the author's hope that this book will help answer that question.

Part I attempts to capture something of the wonder and intricacy of the life cycle of the rainbow trout. The photographs are stills selected from one of the finest films ever made about the trout and the ecosystem in which it lives. This thirty-minute film, entitled *The Way of a Trout,* was made in 1969 by James Wilkie, a brilliant amateur photographer with a deep interest in nature and conservation. Mr. Wilkie donated this film to Trout Unlimited in the hope that it could help to stimulate interest in the organization and its cause. Since then it has been seen by tens of thousands of fishermen, naturalists, conservationists, and schoolchildren. In 1971 it won the Outdoor Writers Association of America "Film of the Year" Award among others. Accompanying the stills is Al Hazzard's text, written especially for this book. Dr. Hazzard is one of this country's foremost fisheries biologists and a long-time member of Trout Unlimited's Board of Scientific Advisers.

Part II draws upon the victories and defeats of one highly successful environmental organization to develop both a framework for action and a battle plan. That organization, Trout Unlimited, is a troop of dedicated fishermen who fight to stop pollution of their favorite fishing streams. Whatever the method—cleanup campaign, public opinion seminar, or legal battle—their efforts in their own special self-interest serve the interests of everyone who depends on clean water. And everyone depends on clean water.

The goal of re-creating a healthful environment is universally obligatory. Under whatever banner we work, whether as campers, canoeists, fishermen, or consumers, this book aims to provide a blueprint to convert concern into effective action.

The author wishes to express his appreciation to Mrs. Frances Tonge and Miss Nikki Lewy for their assistance in the research and writing of this book.

Contents

If a Brook Trout can live in it,
man can probably drink it.

—KENNETH L. REID

part 1
the way of a trout

To most people a woodland stream is a pleasant scene of sun and shadow and rippling water. But to an angler it is a community of many forms of life all centering, in his mind at least, on the most beautiful and aggressive of freshwater fish, the trout.

—FREDERICK O. HUTCHINSON

I⊤ IS ONE of those rare, early spring days in the North Country, and the contemplative angler is resting beside a favorite pool awaiting possible action. He knows the trout are there—huge rainbows freshly run from Lake Superior. Some of the larger pools too will hold over resident fish that are worth catching. Only yesterday he has hooked, played, and carefully released a beautiful two-pound

3

female that he hopes will remain and reach trophy size for a later encounter.

He sits on the log enjoying the sunshine. Being a biologist as well as an angler, his thoughts turn to the hazards of a trout's existence

—from the beginnings of its life to the culmination, a fine fish like the one he has battled so successfully.

In a stretch of stream very like this, several years ago, a male and female met and mated. The cock fish, slightly smaller than the

hen, finds her in the act of selecting a nesting site. After several false tries she begins to dig in earnest in the loose gravel near the tail of the pool just before the water breaks over into the next riffle. Here the stream is just the right depth and the gradient sufficient to ensure proper aeration of the developing eggs.

Turning on her side she vibrates her body close to the bottom, stirring up with her broad spotted tail a great cloud of sand, silt, and

fine gravel which drifts downstream. After a brief pause she is at it again. Several days are required to complete the two-foot-long, ten-inch-deep saucerlike depression.

Meanwhile the vividly colored, hook-jawed male stimulates her efforts by crowding his body against her as she rests. Now and then he will swim above her in short circles, brushing her head and dorsal fin with his body. Courtship is frequently interrupted by the persistent efforts of several smaller males to get into the act. Twice cock fish almost as large as he appear on the scene and a battle royal develops, with biting and slashing attack and defense. Before the end of each spawning season many of the males bear cuts and scars, and the tails of the females are ragged from nest building.

But now the female is satisfied with her work, and the nest is ready. The pair, side by side with vents close together, extrude eggs and milt simultaneously as with open mouths and vibrating bodies they move upstream in the shallow trough the female has created. At this climax the smaller attendant males rush in and join in the act of fertilization. Perhaps this is nature's way of ensuring that all of the eggs will be impregnated. Hatchery men often complain of the apparent infertility of the older bucks and strip the milt from some of the smaller fish to add to that of larger males to improve fertilization.

Almost immediately after the sex act the female begins to stir up the gravel at the head of the nest, and it drifts down to cover the newly deposited eggs which, being slightly heavier than water, have mostly collected in the deepest part of the nest depression. A few are bound to wash over the lip of the nest and are lost, some being eaten by the smaller males—perhaps a reward for their contribution to this most important life process.

After periods of rest the spawning act is repeated. Several days may elapse before the female is completely spent and the eggs are safely deposited in the gravel redd. Here development of the young fish proceeds apace, stimulated by the rising water temperature of the stream.

Immediately after the sperm penetrates the shell and its nucleus joins with that of the egg, cell division starts—2-4-16, in geometric progression—and within a week a suggestion of the form of the fish

appears. In another week or two, depending upon water temperature (the higher the temperature up to the critical limit, the faster the

development), the black eye spots appear and the pulsing heart and much of the rest of the embryonic circulatory system are clearly

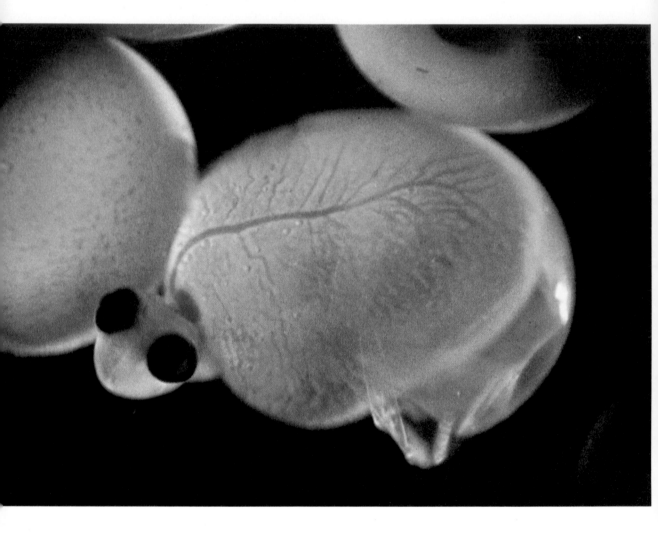

visible through the almost transparent shell. The yolk, which at first makes up most of the egg, becomes less prominent as the embryo grows around it and absorbs this rich food supply.

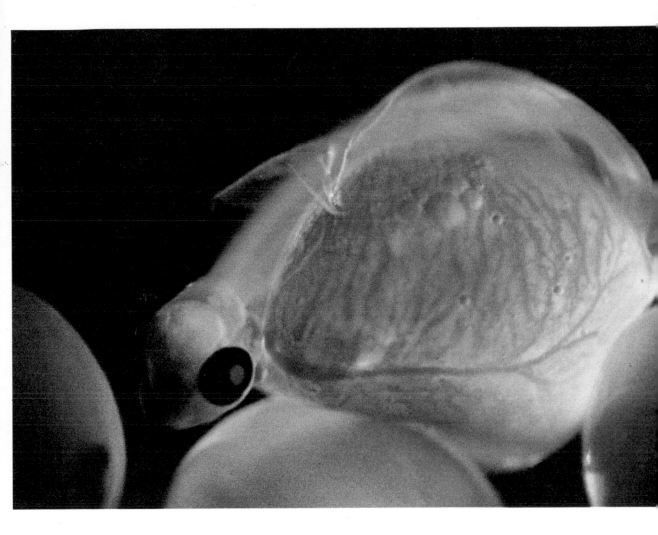

Usually within about six weeks from fertilization, the young trout emerges from the shell. Still weighted down by the attached yolk sack, the newly hatched fry wriggles around among the stones of the nest

depression. A few days more and the young fish has absorbed most of the nourishing burden; the mouth breaks open, and it is able to

16

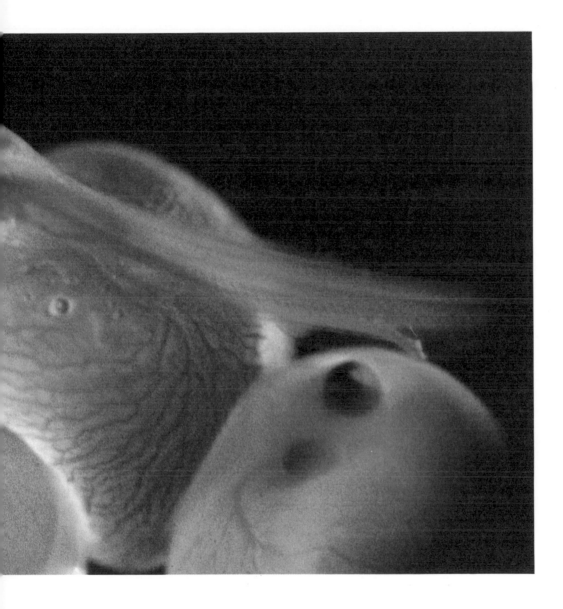

work up through the gravel and swim toward the surface. At this stage the little ones collect in the quieter, silt-bottomed areas along the

stream margins, where a good food supply in the form of tiny midge larvae and crustaceans is brought to them by the gentle currents.

Although most of the eggs which became safely buried in the redd
were fertilized and develop, many never reach the free-swimming fry

stage. Livestock or fishermen wading through the nesting area may kill the developing eggs, especially during the tender stage before the

eye spots appear. Silt-laden waters from poorly protected watersheds are particularly damaging to the buried eggs and may smother all of them. Some may be lost to insects, crayfish, and to fish such as the sculpins or to suckers that may work over the gravel beds in their own spawning activities.

The fry which develop successfully and make it to the stream margins are faced with other hazards. Predacious insects, such as the water scorpion, lie in wait for the unwary young. Other fish, oc-

casionally including larger trout, may account for additional losses among survivors of the subterranean period of existence.

As the fry grow and reach fingerling size, still other perils await them—some from the world above the surface, some from below. The

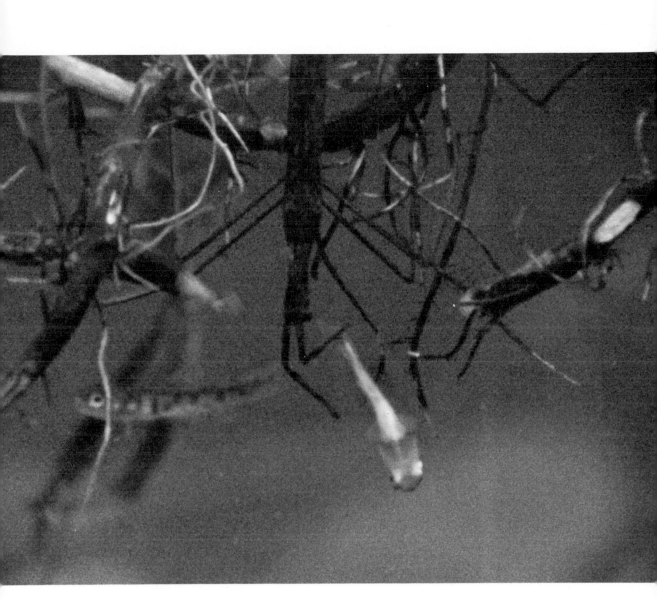

kingfisher perched on the overhanging tree limb waits to drop like a stone to grasp the unwary young trout in his tweezerlike bill. But not every dive is successful, and if fish other than trout are present he is just as likely to take them as the fish in which the angler

28

is interested. Some fishermen hate the kingfisher, but what would a trout stream be like without his cheerful rattle?

The green heron may consume some young trout, although its food usually consists of frogs, insects, and warm-water fishes com-

mon to the marshy areas which it frequents. But in the unnatural situation of a hatchery pond, which attracts all kinds of birds, snakes, and mammals that feed on fish, this bird as well as its large relative, the great blue heron, may account for many trout.

Stalking cautiously through a shallow area or waiting motionless at a likely spot, the heron spears its prey by a lightning thrust of the bill and, flipping the stunned fish about, deftly swallows it whole.

Even more destructive to larger trout, including those of the size

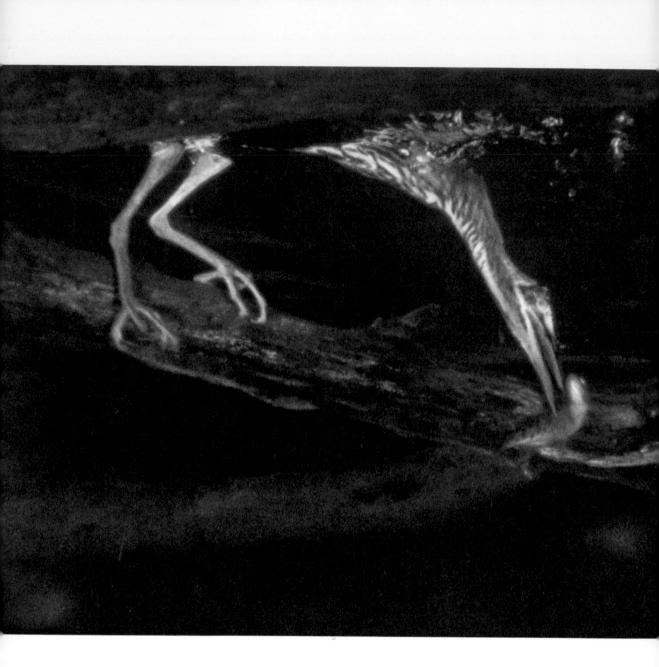

to interest the angler, may be the American merganser. This "fish
duck" has been found to be a serious predator on many Canadian
trout and salmon streams; these birds concentrate also on spring-fed

sections of trout streams during winter months when the lower river courses freeze. Several Michigan rivers, such as the Au Sable, attract to their headwaters large numbers of these birds, which have been

found to feed heavily on trout up to sixteen inches in length. Hatchery rearing ponds which may be ice-free during these extreme periods of cold have also been the objects of merganser raids, with sizable losses of large fish reported. An expert diver and underwater swimmer, the merganser can catch even the fastest trout. The serrated bill and flexible mouth are adapted to seizing and gulping down large fish. It is indeed fortunate that most of the waters frequented by the merganser are dominated by fish other than trout. Predators (except for man) are usually not selective in their feeding but rather are opportunists, taking the most available prey.

Water snakes are common along many trout streams, and I have seen snapping turtles in the crystal-clear waters of the Pigeon River in Michigan. Although suckers and minnows make up a larger share of the fish diet of water snakes than do trout, and aquatic vegetation is much more common than fish in snapping turtles' stomachs, many sportsmen resent their presence also.

Fishermen themselves may on occasion unwittingly contribute to the toll of predation, as witness the trout which has unsuspectingly taken a worm dangled in front of it by a freckle-faced farm boy with his cane pole and bobber. But his line is not strong enough to handle

the active fish and breaks in the struggle. Fish and bobber disappear as the disappointed lad trudges home to repair his outfit. What of the trout now tethered to this annoying appendage that it cannot discard

and that any moment may become entangled in the submerged brush
of the pool, exposing the trout to attack from many sources?

An otter may be the first to be attracted to the struggling fish.

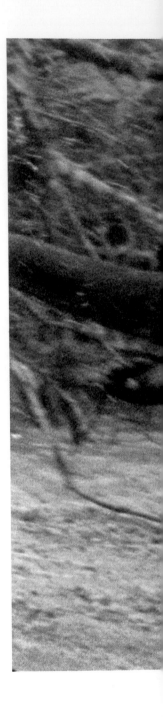

It glides through the water almost as easily as a trout. Except for its need to surface for air, it is completely at home in the water. Once rare,

it is now quite common along many trout streams. The sight of an otter with its cubs playfully battling the waves of a small isolated bog

43

lake in upper Michigan has been for me a small but persistently comforting memory. On another occasion I had a close-up view of an otter along the South Branch of the Au Sable in an area where the marsh marigolds were in full bloom on both sides of this lovely trout stream.

But consider the predicament of our big trout tethered by tangled line and bobber, an easy prey to this hungry predator. Fortunately the line breaks again in the struggle and the freed fish readily evades the otter; the hook, again by good luck, is caught only in the lip and soon works out, perhaps leaving a wiser trout.

The story could well have ended differently if the worm had been swallowed. The anatomy of the trout is such that the heart is literally in the throat region. With the point of the hook down, there is a good chance that it will pierce the gullet and penetrate the liver and the heart. If the point is up, the kidney and brain are vulnerable. The delicate gills with their array of large blood vessels tend to entangle the hook if the point is turned to either side when the fisherman strikes. Extensive hooking experiments in Michigan and more recently elsewhere have demonstrated conclusively the mortality caused by natural bait of any kind, regardless of hook size or the care used in releasing the fish. Over 33 percent trout hooked on bait die as contrasted with a mortality of about 3 percent for artificial flies. Later tests have shown that unbaited spinners, plugs, and spoons, even with treble hooks, are barely more lethal than flies. If a lure can be readily swallowed—and even artificial flies are sometimes sucked in deep when trout are feeding ravenously—the chances are good that an undersized fish will be killed sooner or later. This is particularly true on heavily fished public waters where repeated hookings of small fish are likely. It is a potent argument for no size limits on waters not restricted to artificial lures.

Another predator that might easily have caught the tethered trout is the mink. It is common along most trout streams and is not averse to a meal of fish. Like the otter, its favorite food is the crayfish, but fish remains are not uncommon in its scats. Even though this animal may take some trout, I would hate to see the mink eliminated

from our trout waters. I am glad that it is so wary and hard to trap. I will never forget an experience on the headwaters of the White River in Michigan a few years ago. It was late in a summer's afternoon and I was resting on a stream-bank log—one of many abandoned in the lumbering drives of years ago—waiting for the evening rise. Around the bend and along the edge of the far shore appeared what seemed to be a long brown animal. This soon resolved itself into a mink followed head to tail by four young, which undulated in and out of the overhanging bank until they were out of sight. I can't recall now whether fishing was good or poor that day or how many trout I caught, but that unusual streamside picture is etched in my memory.

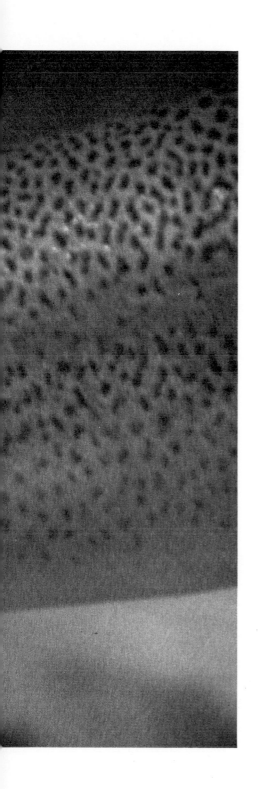

But to get back to our two-pound female rainbow. One of the few survivors of a spawning act such as we have just described, she has successfully avoided the many hazards of a precarious existence. I recall the words of my old Cornell professor. We had been discussing the rate of survival of the eggs produced by a mature trout. Assuming a fully stocked stream, he said, of the many thousands spawned during a trout's lifetime only two eggs need to develop and become mature fish in order to maintain the same number of fish or, in modern terms, have "zero population growth." Our fish is now the undisputed queen of this remote pool. Here in the slow current behind a fallen willow tree where insects float within easy reach, she will grow to trophy size.

The angler approaches the pool carefully from below, avoiding the slippery log that had been his undoing in an earlier attempt to reach the proper spot from which to present his fly. But again he is distracted by the sights and sounds of the enchanting woodland setting. A large green frog is croaking in hopes of attracting a mate. In a nearby pond the sound of the spring peepers almost drowns out the lovely trill of the mating toads. The warming sun has also brought out a dragonfly, whose zooming attempts to capture nearby mosquitoes the angler appreciates. A turtle sunning itself on a log slips noiselessly into the water at his approach.

The trailing arbutus along the nearby wooded bank, whose delicate form and color and delicious fragrance the angler had enjoyed

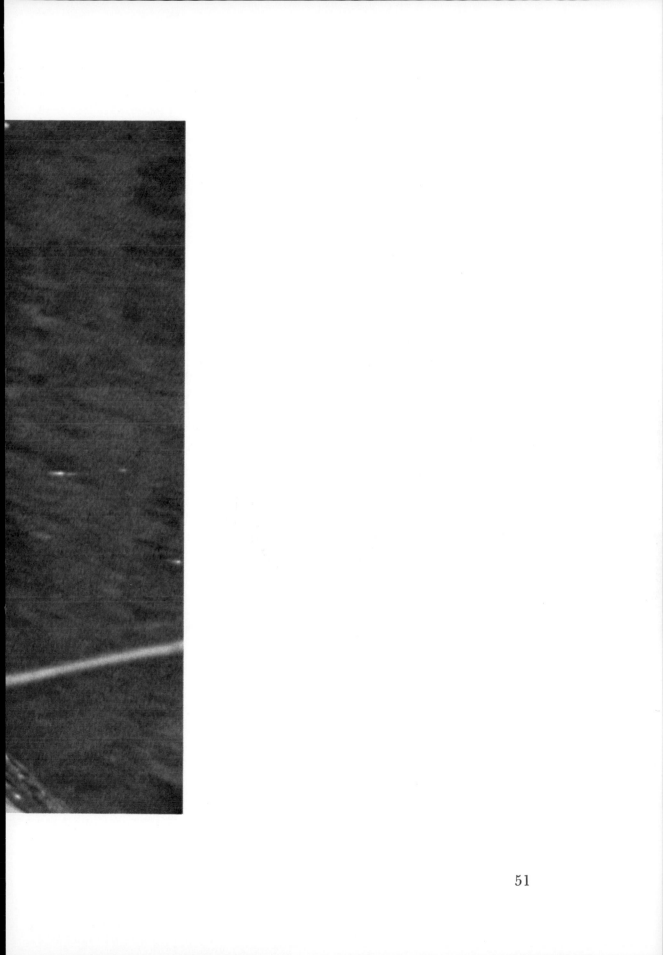

on his earlier visit to the stream, has now passed its peak but the
Juneberry, called shadbush in many areas, is now in full bloom.
Anticipation of the sight of these delicate white blooms, appearing to
be a pale pink in the variety where the new leaves come out with the
flowers, was one of the reasons for the timing of this particular fishing
trip. Also the angler knows that some of the best fly fishing comes

with the peak of the shadbush bloom. It is then that many of the early mayflies begin their emergence.

The patron saint of angling, Sir Izaak Walton, long ago expressed the present homely saying that "It's not all fishing to fish" in the more elegant language of his day. He said, "I will walk the meadows by some gliding stream and there contemplate the lilies that

take no care and those very many other living creatures that are not only created but fed, man knows not how, by the God of Nature."

The angler's reverie on the beauties of nature and the writers who have so well portrayed the charms of his favorite sport is interrupted by a sudden splash just ahead of the fallen willow. A big rainbow is starting to feed on the mayflies which have begun to appear on the water and, caught in the eddy, are drifting over her lie. These are adult flies that emerged yesterday after a year in the silty gravel of the stream margin. They have rested on the overhanging bushes while transforming to the imago stage and are now mating above the water. The males, spent after this final flight, and the females, to deposit their eggs, drop to the water surface in the last acts of their ephemeral existence. It is a thrilling sight for the angler to witness, and when the mating flight comes early in the afternoon, as in this case, it provides the finest fly fishing of the season.

The angler wades out to where he can pick up some of the dying insects in his hand and carefully examines them. He searches his fly box for an imitation but finds just one that suits him—and, he hopes, the trout. He carefully ties it on, testing the leader to be sure it is sound, for he knows that it must be perfect if it is to hold this giant fish. Carefully he moves out into the stream until he is in the proper position. Several false casts dry the fly and extend the line to the correct distance. The cast would have been perfect except that a sudden gust of wind causes the line to lodge in a drooping hemlock to his rear. He hopes a stout tug will dislodge the fly, but when the leader comes down the handsome artificial lure is missing. In vain he tries fly after fly from his box. Then, realizing that he must "match the hatch" for this selectively feeding trout, he retires to the bank where

he can tie a proper imitation. Thankful that he has his portable fly-tying kit with him, he clamps the vise to a tree and, selecting the correct materials, soon produces another good imitation of the mayflies that are attracting the big rainbow. It is ready for the test.

This time he is more careful with his back cast, and the fly drops lightly above the rising trout. It must look just right to the fish; she sucks it in, and the fight is on, the typical rainbow battle with many jumps and thrilling runs. The tackle holds and the angler is skillful

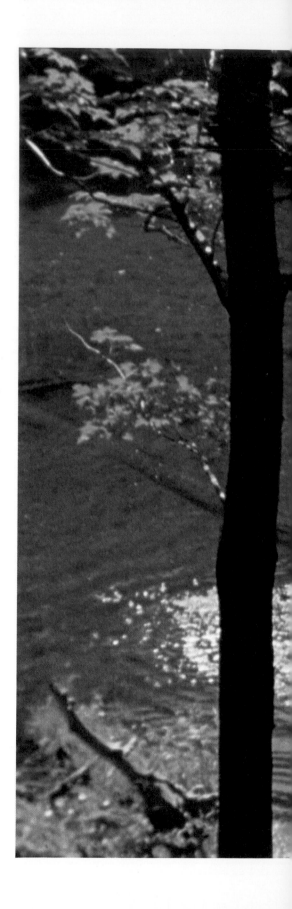

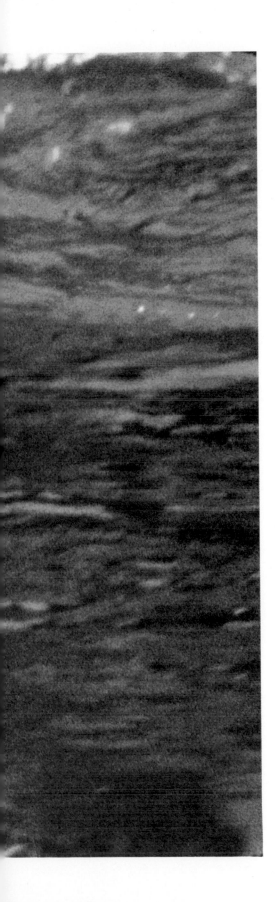

in keeping the fish away from the submerged logs and out from under the willow's entangling roots. He exerts the right amount of pressure to hold the fish without breaking the slender tippet.

Finally the great trout tires and the angler slides her to the shore, where, with one hand holding the leader and the other around the base of the broad tail, he contemplates his prize. It is a magnificent

trout and it has been a thrilling contest. But should he kill it?

Like the angler in the film, he thinks of the thousands of eggs she may produce in future years and the other great fish that may be her offspring, and he remembers the comment of the narrator, Frederick Hutchinson, that "all of its enemies except one must destroy the trout to live—only man has an alternative."

With no regrets the angler gently releases her, and she slips back into the pool.

part 2
the battle

1. know the enemy

WHEN THE WHITE MAN first arrived in North America, he found the woodlands teeming with wildlife, the waterways with fish. It seemed there could never be an end to this plenty. And there needn't have been. Fisheries and forests have the ability to renew themselves forever as long as the ecosystem remains balanced.

But "ecosystem" was not part of the frontier vocabulary. Instead, the first settlers developed the philosophy of "use, abuse, and move on" which followed them from sea to shining sea. Behind them, an ever-widening wake of fouled waters testified to their ignorance.

The time is past when ignorance can excuse polluted waterways. Certainly the early settlers had little foreknowledge of what their destruction would mean to generations unborn. Today we are all too painfully aware of the consequences of unbridled industrial and municipal discharges, the thoughtless damming of free-flowing rivers, and the mismanagement of watersheds. But violators persist, motivated by greed or blinded by myopia. Mining companies gouge the earth and drain by-product acid into mountain streams. Government agencies build billion-dollar hydroelectric projects that block spawning grounds. Timber firms log forests, leaving debris and whole hillsides to wash away. They are all guilty, but no more than the citizen who sanctions their destruction for short-term financial gain.

Effective counteraction begins with identification. If the Enemy is known, his actions are suspect. Agencies or organizations with a tradition of despoliation are the first places environmental allies should look to prevent more destruction. It is ironic that perhaps the greatest threat to our natural resources comes from mechanisms set up to protect it.

The U.S. Army Corps of Engineers, the Bureau of Reclamation, the U.S. Forest Service, even the Tennessee Valley Authority, have all served their country well. Now, except for the Forest Service, they prolong their viability only at environmental cost. (The Forest Service is faulted specifically for its mismanagement.) Because of the magnitude of the bureaucratic threat, these primary culprits will be discussed separately.

The Army Corps of Engineers

The U.S. Army Corps of Engineers has worked hard to earn the title of "Public Enemy Number One," Justice William O. Douglas's epithet for these busy little beavers. One hundred and fifty years and $21.5 billion have left the Corps virtual masters of spoiling the unspoiled. A flood anywhere in the United States brings Corps engineers and operatives hard upon its receding waters. Their panacea? "Build a dam!"

The Corps' instinct for dam-building left one western fisherman afraid to leave his garden hose running in the back yard; he said he feared they would arrive at his front door with orders to impound the water. So far, he has been lucky.

The Columbia and Snake rivers have not. Once these clear, rushing waters hosted the finest salmon and steelhead runs in the world. Now fourteen dams stand between the adult Pacific salmon and their spawning ground on the Upper Snake. The first dams on the Columbia provided no fish bypasses, and though some were installed later, they are still not negotiable by all fish, many of which lose their way in slack-water reservoirs that are without guiding currents. The Grand Coulee Dam alone isolated salmon and steelhead from hundreds of miles of spawning gravel because it was not considered economical to build fish ladders.

Fishways, however, are far from the only problem. The artificially impounded waters of the reservoirs hold summer heat up to a month longer than free-flowing streams. The abnormal warmth heightens disease, promotes the growth of algae and fungi, and encourages the in-migration of trash fish.

A Federally sponsored study at the Bonneville Fish Hatchery showed the incidence of disease in salmon rose from 10 to 90 percent as water temperatures rose from 50 to 62 degrees. In late summer and fall, temperatures over 68 degrees were recorded all along the Columbia system. The Bonneville study reported 100 percent mortality at that temperature.

The once-crystal waters of the Snake are now the color of pea soup, green with the slime of algae. The warm water of the reservoirs causes the decomposition of aquatic growth, a process which reduces oxygen levels and suffocates the fish. The tastes and odors of decay have forced at least one city, Twin Falls, Idaho, to abandon the Snake as a source of municipal water.

The deliberate inundation of orchard land adds the residue of tons of DDT to the reservoir's storehouse. In addition, flooding old mining and pulp mill sites contribute poisonous methyl mercury. As a result, the Idaho Fish and Game Department suggests that certain species of fish from the Brownlee and American Falls reservoir are unfit for human consumption.

But the real killer is "gas bubble disease." For years no one could explain why masses of migrant salmon floated eyeless below the dams. In spring, 1970, an estimated 2.8 million chinook salmon and 43,000 fish other than salmon were killed. The following year a repeat performance claimed more. Cause: unknown.

Finally, research revealed the answer—nitrogen supersaturation. To prevent the fish from passing through the turbines of the dams, the Corps channeled them instead over the empty spillways of unused generator bays (empty because the need for hydroelectric power was insufficient to warrant installing turbines in more than half the available bays). As the water rushed over the steep concrete cliffs, nitrogen was forced into solution at rates higher than 100 percent, a situation that occurs in natural waterfalls. Unlike nature's tumbling rapids that dissipate excess nitrogen, slack-water reservoirs hold it to fatal levels.

In a process analogous to the bends of deep-sea divers, nitrogen enters the fish as it swims through deep water and expands as the fish enter shallower water. Low-level supersaturation causes ruptures just below the fish's skin which increases its susceptibility to infection. At higher levels, the pressure of the expanding gas causes massive internal bleeding and forces the fish's eyes to burst. Surviving salmon and steelhead beat themselves to death on artificial barriers they can no longer see.

Turbines would have claimed 95 percent of the downstream migrants. This way the dams only get 70 to 85 percent. In an effort to reduce the figure still further, the Corps is experimenting with mechanical devices that break the rush of water over the spillways. Until the devices prove sufficient, some salmon and steelhead are trucked overland to below the affected areas. (Nitrogen supersaturation has been recorded as much as 400 miles into the Pacific.) Hatcheries are cooperating with the Corps to release fish during periods of low supersaturation. But the problem is far from solved.

With solutions pending, the fish kills continue and the Snake gets ever greener, but the Corps of Engineers keeps damming. Four dams were originally proposed for the Lower Snake, to make inland ports of two cities 470 miles from the sea. The barge traffic that the project was designed thirty-five years ago to accommodate has all but disappeared, due to competitive railroad and trucking rates. Two suits have been filed to halt construction of the Lower Granite dam, the only dam of the four that remains uncompleted; one by the Northwest Steelheaders Council of TU and the other by the State of Washington, which asks $82 million in damages, the estimated value of the steelhead loss. But construction goes on.

The Bureau of Reclamation

Limited to only fourteen western states and Hawaii, the Bureau of Reclamation runs second to the Army Corps of Engineers for total appropriations. They take a tip, however, from a popular car rental agency and "try harder." Many water-short municipalities in the West still regard the BuRec as the quickest funnel to the public treasury. And they are probably right.

Bureau projects do have a relatively easy legislative time in both the Senate and the House. Proposals go first to the Interior and Insular Affairs committees. The Senate's committee sits Reclamation states in all but two of its sixteen seats, the House committee in all but six of its thirty-eight.

Nonetheless, a completed project does the same environmental damage whether the dam was built by the Bureau of Reclamation or the Army Corps of Engineers. The problems of thermal pollution, eutrophication, and nitrogen supersaturation are endemic to the dam, not the agency that builds them. What makes Bureau projects particularly reprehensible is that most of them are quite unnecessary.

The Bureau of Reclamation's principal activity is providing water for irrigation. Existing food surpluses already cost millions of dollars in storage every year and make one third of the available croplands in this country dispensable. Predictions indicate that these surpluses can only increase. By 1980, two thirds of today's farms will be well on their way to oblivion, but the Bureau will probably be busy making more.

Since 1905, their Derby Dam has diverted water from the Truckee River for the Newlands Reclamation Project in Nevada. Pyramid Lake, whose only source of water is the Truckee, has supplied fish for generations of Northern Paiute Indians. Three quarters of the tribe's total income is earned by selling fishing and boating privileges on the lake, which borders their reservation.

Every year the water level drops another foot and the shoreline recedes another ten feet. Now that the lake's surface is fifty square miles smaller than it was in 1905, sandbars have appeared at its south end to block trout from their spawning gravels on the Truckee. Receding waters increase salinity, and the fish are dying. With them goes the Northern Paiutes' principal means of livelihood.

The Indians never approved the Newlands Project; they were not even consulted. In 1963, when they learned another project would divert still more water from Pyramid Lake, they objected strenuously. Interior Secretary Stewart L. Udall placated the tribe with promises that the Department would act in their behalf. His successor, Secretary Walter J. Hickel, also assured the Indians that their lake would not be destroyed. Then he approved a proposal to "stabilize" Pyramid Lake by lowering it another 152 feet.

In Idaho, BuRec's Lower Teton Project calls for the erection of a 300-foot dam in a 250-foot canyon through which flows twenty-seven beautiful miles of the Teton River. The canyon provides a critical winter range for elk and deer and a year-round habitat for river otter, wild bobcat, and ruffed grouse. The relatively inaccessible river's deep pools and riffles sustain a healthy population of native cutthroat trout.

The productivity of fishing waters is greatly reduced by siltation resulting from various land and water projects such as road construction and channel alteration *(Colorado Wildlife Division)*.

Damage to streams can result from logging practices and attempts to clear out debris *(California Department of Fish and Game)*.

Placer and strip-mining create mass destruction of surface areas and streams
(Idaho Fish and Game Department).

It takes channeled streams seventy years to recover about 20 percent of their former productivity *(Georgia Game and Fish Commission)*.

A water diversion for power generation completely dewaters a portion of the Colorado River near Glenwood Springs, Colorado *(Robert L. Hoover)*.

In spite of public indignation, John Martin Reservoir in Colorado was drained three times in a ten-year period, resulting in heavy fish losses *(Colorado Wildlife Division)*.

The dam will raise the high-water level almost to the canyon's rim. The elk and deer will die; the other animals will disappear. The fish have already felt the dam's destruction, and construction hasn't yet begun.

In 1962, before the Bureau finished its detailed investigation of the Lower Teton Project, a February flood brought speedy Congressional authorization. This was for a standard irrigation dam. Only this time, the BuRec project would provide supplemental irrigation water for land now using double the state allotment and initial irrigation water for another 37,000 acres, half of which were already receiving water from private pumping facilities.

Four months before Congress appropriated $10 million to start digging, the BuRec constructed an access road with 6,000 to 7,000 yards of gravel they dredged from the Lower Teton River. Fishery biologists from Idaho Fish and Game reported that severe silting had resulted.

Outraged fishermen and conservationists succeeded in bringing Interior Secretary Rogers Morton to the dam site. After a complete project review, he recommended scrapping the project. But President Nixon overrode Morton's recommendation and issued a news release indicating that after an exhaustive investigation the Department of the Interior wholeheartedly approved the Lower Teton Dam.

Once again TU and its allies filed suit. And, again, the lengthy process of appeals began. But for the Bureau of Reclamation, like the Army Corps of Engineers, the dam must go on.

The Tennessee Valley Authority

The Tennessee Valley Authority is probably the most autonomous and difficult to catch of all environmental enemies. A baby of the Depression thirties, the TVA has roamed the mountain valleys of the Southeast until many rivers show not a single mile of free-flowing water. With little left to do, its budgets get bigger each year and its office carpets get thicker. TVA seems to enjoy an immunity in the halls of Congress that leaves its appropriations virtually unassailable.

It saw the opportunity for a $41-million project in the last thirty-three free-flowing miles of the Little Tennessee or, as it is affectionately known, the Little T. Since the mid-sixties, the people of Tennessee have tried to fend off the Tellico Project. Finally, in January, 1972, they were successful in getting a court order to temporarily halt construction (see Chapter 2). But until the case is permanently settled, the proposed project is illustrative of TVA destruction.

At present, four dams have obliterated all but these last few miles of the Little T. Somehow, despite the other dams that span its breadth, this free-flowing section is remarkably cold and pure. It offers fishermen the double thrill of float fishing and challenging rainbows and browns.

The project calls for the construction of a reservoir with an industrially developed shoreline. The warm water of the reservoir will have an even more difficult time diluting and disposing of the resulting industrial wastes than would cold water. What industry doesn't do, the TVA will. A canal running from the Tellico Reservoir to Fort Loudon Lake will carry with it the waste of the most severely polluted project in the TVA system.

The Tellico project will inundate the sacred capital city of the Cherokees, archaeological sites dating back 8,000 years, and agricultural and forest land. Prerevolutionary Fort Loudon will be preserved on an island in the middle of a lake accessible only by boat or bridge. However, if the reservoir's pollution levels reach as high as predicted, it may not be unrealistic to expect the landmark to become altogether inaccessible.

The future of the rainbows and browns is not a matter of conjecture. Their survival in the warm, polluted Tellico reservoir will be impossible. Tennessee will lose probably its finest cold-water fishery. But the TVA will chalk up another "success."

Because of the delicate interdependence of trees and water, forestry policies determine watershed quality. The Forest Service has earned the name of Enemy by destroying both. This guardian of Smokey the Bear and 187 million acres of national forest ignores the directives that empower it in the first place. The Multiple Use and Sustained Yield Act trusts the Service to provide timber, forage, recreation, wildlife management, and stream protection in a way that ensures their continuation forever. However, shortsightedness has forced the Forest Service to view its role as timber harvester, not protector.

Since 1950, the amount of timber cut in national forests has doubled. Replanting has not. As a result, 18 million acres of productive lands are either bare or producing half their potential. Photographers must look longer and harder for the calendar shots they used to find without difficulty. No one wants to look at an eroded hillside for "January," but the unfortunate fact is that too many acres of woodland look that way year round.

Carelessly constructed access roads wash topsoil and timber debris into streams. Logs are yarded through shallow waterways, destroying gravel beds. And the most destructive method of all, clearcutting, removed *all* the trees on one third of the logged areas of the West in 1969. There, in the Rocky Mountains, reforestation of clearcuts is singularly unsuccessful. Some treeless cuts of ten and fifteen years ago still grow only meadow grass even after four attempts to replant.

Clear-cutting leaves barren soil with no root system to hold it in place. Resulting runoffs increase the natural rate of erosion as much as five times. Sediment then clogs streams, chokes vegetations, and destroys spawning grounds. When the Oregon State Game Commission studied the effect of clear-cutting on only one half mile of stream in the Alsea watershed, they found a 24-degree difference in water temperature before and after logging and three quarters of the local cutthroat trout dead. Four years later, the trout population had not returned to pre-logging levels. It is difficult to imagine the effect of clear-cutting on 1,000 acres, as was practiced on the Bitterroot Forest of Montana.

Miscellaneous Enemies

These agencies are not the only ones hacking away at natural resources. There are others holding lesser positions only because their targets are local or regional in scope. Water conservation districts, irrigation companies, municipalities, and developers are all responsible to one degree or another for the destruction of the environment and, with it, free-flowing rivers and fisheries. Some are even legally protected in their destruction.

A hundred-year-old mining law puts mining operations beyond governmental control. Unlike the oil and gas industries, which lease their land, mining companies are permitted to claim land in the public domain as long as they "develop its potential." Ironically, the more limited the potential, the greater the destruction. The cheapest way of mining is also the most destructive.

Strip-mining, the mineral equivalent of clear-cutting, is used to mine ore of borderline economic value. To uncover the ore, the earth is cut open in great strips. The rate of erosion doubles and quadruples. Washed-away soil carries with it acid mine drainage. Wildlife habitats are destroyed and the polluted water will no longer sustain fish or healthy aquatic life. Yet the mineral potential for which this environmental damage is done may often be considerably lower than that of the local auto wrecking yard.

In 1970, 3.5 million acres were strip-mined. The National Coal Association reported reclaiming only about 500,000 acres (and it must be noted that their standard of reclamation is rarely as high as that of concerned, or even unconcerned, citizens). Effective reclamation, though it may restore aesthetics, has proven unable to undo the damage done to affected waterways.

Channeled streams have a slightly brighter future; rather than being permanently sterilized, they recover about 20 percent of their former productivity seventy years after channeling. Within the last few years the Soil Conservation Service has straightened 6,000 miles of streams and rivers in the United States. The process entails stripping vegetation from the sloping riverbanks and replacing it with concrete sides that direct the water along a more favorable course.

One of the Service's more stunning efforts concerned the Tippah River in Mississippi. Before channeling, the meandering Tippah held more than 240 pounds of fish per acre. Straightened, it contained 4.8 pounds per acre. Nonetheless, Congress has already authorized another 12,000 miles of Tippah-like ditches.

Rivaling the Soil Conservation with its disastrous policies, the Denver Water Board must be included in any listing of environmental enemies. With a little help from its friends, the Army Corps of Engineers and the Bureau of Reclamation, the Board extended its influence almost to World Court, where a threatened suit by the Mexican government followed from its mismanagement of Colorado rivers.

A 1944 treaty promised Mexico an annual 1.5 million acre-feet of irrigation water. (An acre-foot is the amount of water necessary to cover one acre of land to a depth of one foot.) However, the Colorado River, which eventually fulfills that contract, is overcommitted upstream in Denver Water Board territory. For every 100 acre-feet of available water, 125 are pledged to industrial, municipal, and agricultural uses. The Denver Water Board continues to pledge more, counting on additional dam projects to help meet the contracts.

These dams divert fresh water from the Lower Basin states and Mexico. As it is used again and again, the water continually picks up dissolved salt and minerals. By 1961, the salinity level of the water finally delivered to 310,000 Mexicans was so high it couldn't be used for irrigation, let alone drinking. There is no need to recount the effect on cold-water fisheries.

At every turn the Enemy attacks natural resources. These projects, large and small, for whatever purpose, disrupt a precariously balanced ecosystem. Man is part of nature's interlocking complexities, but only a part. His survival depends on his ability to maintain the balance, not destroy it.

2. know the facts

CONCERN MAY BE the prime mover in joining the battle to save the environment, but facts are the weapons that win the war. All the emotionalism of "Save the Earth" and "God and Nature" will never penetrate the armor of a project's feasibility study. Some studies cost millions of dollars and take years to prepare. The only way to discredit one and ultimately dump a project is to know more about it than the project's backers.

Although the task is tedious and time-consuming, it is absolutely essential. Three things favor the environmentalist: (1) the dedication and diverse expertise of his allies, (2) his dealing in fact versus the Enemy's dealing in projections, and (3) the axiomatic truth that the hare runs faster for his life than the fox for his supper. The battle is, after all, one of survival.

Victories are doubly important because each one makes the next battle easier to win. Until recent years, most projects went uncontested, except for an occasional jab at padded budgets. But with growing environmental awareness, projects which threaten destruction have an increasingly difficult time. Congressional project boosters are matched by conscientious senators, agency functionaries by diligent conservationists. Formerly unquestioned enemies are not only questioned but sometimes stopped cold. The action, which impairs forever their destructive potential, begins far away from the halls of Congress, with a concerned ex-forester in Montana or a handful of historians and dedicated fishermen in Tennessee.

The Bitterroot Forest Controversy

The grade-school text that tells of the scrupulous forester who marks only mature trees for cutting might well be describing G. M. "Brandy" Brandborg, supervisor of the Bitterroot National Forest in Montana for twenty years before his retirement in 1955. Brandy practiced "selective cutting" even when other foresters yielded to the newer methods.

Throughout the late forties and fifties and early sixties, wages soared. To remain competitive in the marketplace, lumber companies found it imperative to cut the cost of operation. They developed massive machinery that made it possible to cut more acres faster and cheaper. Marketable timber was logged. The rest was left to rot, choked with debris, or piled in massive windrows and burned. At that time, the only groups who pressured the Forest Service coveted its timber. In the absence of counterpressure, their demands were met. Larger and larger tracts were cut, on steeper slopes, even adjacent to live water, but no one complained.

Until Brandborg retired, these destructive practices never got a foothold in the Bitterroot. Once he was no longer supervisor, however, they ravaged the forest. Nothing was visible from the highway, where most people viewed the Bitterroot. But inside, where Brandborg still liked to wander, clear-cuts scarred whole mountainsides.

The former forester became increasingly vocal over the degradation of his forest. A young environmental writer, Dale Burk of the *Daily Missoulian,* picked up his distress cries. Burk published Brandborg's findings that 25 million board feet of ponderosa pine had been logged annually since the 1970 allowable cut was set at 18.3 million board feet. Brandborg maintained that the Ponderosa Pine Management Plan, drawn up in 1941 and allowing 7.5 million board feet to be cut each year, was still valid. The Bitterroot Forest Service admitted to clear-cutting approximately 11,000 acres, nearly half the total logged area of the Bitterroot between 1964 and 1969, but to planting or seeding only 10,067 acres. Throughout the West, Burk's syndicated column carried Brandborg's dismal predictions that such practices doomed the forest.

While the *Daily Missoulian* was angering men to action, Bitterroot Valley ranchers joined the fray. Alarmed by decreasing stream flows in the summer and damaging runoffs in the spring, the ranchers banded together, along with Brandborg's son, Stewart, Executive Director of the Wilderness Society, and Otto Teller, of Trout Unlimited. These "Madmen from Montana," as they were known to the Forest Service, focused national attention on the Bitterroot Forest. (Their methods will be detailed in Chapter 5.)

The Forest Service was forced to dispatch a special study team to evaluate forestry practices on the Bitterroot. Cognizant of the old "study commission silencing trick," conservationists commissioned their own group of professional foresters to do a parallel study. Dr. Arnold Bolle, Dean of the School of Forestry at the University of Montana, headed a group of six of his colleagues.

The Forest Service's task force reported:

We can not support the claim that the approved allowable cut for the forest is too high. However, the actual cut of ponderosa pine during the past few years has been too heavy because the allowable cut calculations for that species were misinterpreted. Moreover, the total cut of all species has been slightly above the approved cut.

The Bolle Commission found that "slightly above the approved cut" meant 37.2 million board feet between 1966 and 1969. The Commission confirmed Brandborg's initial charge that neither multiple use nor sustained yield was practiced in the Bitterroot. Its Statement of Findings included the following:

Multiple use management, in fact, does not exist as the governing principle of the Bitterroot National Forest.

Quality timber management and harvest practices are missing. Consideration of recreation, watershed, wildlife and grazing appear as afterthoughts.

The management sequence of clear-cutting—terracing—planting cannot be justified as an investment for producing timber on the Bitterroot National Forest. We doubt that the Bitterroot National Forest can continue to produce timber at the present harvest level.

The statement concluded that the management practices of the Bitterroot put it "completely out of step with the interests and desires of the American people." Montana Senator Lee Metcalf entered the Bolle Report in the *Congressional Record*.

Armed with the Bolle Report and national attention, conservationists prevented passage of the Timber Supply Act of 1970. The law, designed to validate presently illegal lumbering procedures, never got out of committee. Its defeat led the way for the introduction of protective legislation and brought industry to the bargaining table. Working with conservationists, many firms are now seeking to devise programs which will meet the needs of both groups.

The Bitterroot got a new regional forester. Among his first acts was the banning of clear-cutting on any area under his direct control without complete study and review. Improved road-building methods were instituted to prevent environmental damage. Orders were given forbidding cutting on or through live waters and on unusually steep slopes. Most important for the continuation of the Bitterroot, greater emphasis was placed on replanting. The Multiple Use and Sustained Yield Act again became the rule of the forest.

The success of the Madmen from Montana spread to other states. Wyoming conducted in-house investigations of four of its forests. A West Virginia legislative commission looked into charges of mismanagement in its Monongahela National Forest. Additional studies may force the entire Forest Service to reconfirm its establishing principles and, at last, manage all the forest for all the people.

The Tellico Project

The Tennessee Valley Authority expected no trouble with its $41-million prospect (now probably $69-million) of converting thirty-three miles of the Little T into 16,000 acres of slack water. "No trouble" became a six-year fight. The battle lines drew up: on one side, the TVA led by Director Aubrey J. Wagner, called by the *Knoxville Journal* the czar of Tennessee water resources; on the other, forty-three organizations joined in a coalition actively opposed to the Tellico Project. The list, which has lengthened since the mid-sixties when the battle began, includes groups as divergent as the Tennessee Society of the Daughters of the American Revolution, the Cherokee Nation, Trout Unlimited, and the Sweetwater Valley Feeder Pig Association.

Pleas to preserve the cold-water fish, the forts, and the archaeological sites served only to anger Wagner to speechmaking and foot-stomping. The Coalition turned its efforts instead to fact-finding. By discrediting the TVA's projected benefits, they succeeded in securing an injunction, temporarily halting construction until the case can be permanently resolved.

First, the Coalition dealt with the reasons for building the dam.

The TVA said it would breathe new life into a dying area by encouraging industrial development. The facts disclosed that the criterion of industrial development was added only when the traditional triple entente of navigation, flood control, and power production failed to justify the project. According to the nine banks serving the affected area, the "failing economy" had actually increased its deposits 74 percent in the six years prior to the project's proposal. Farm product sales increased 40 percent from 1955 to 1960, and the percentage of people on welfare fell below both state and national averages.

Notwithstanding environmental losses, which were never tabulated, the project counted $710,000 annual benefits in "shoreline development." For twenty years the threat of a dam prevented industry from locating along this portion of the Little T for fear of being inundated. In the meantime, the firms had located elsewhere. When an independent agency in Washington, D.C., studied the Tellico Project's potential for industrialization, they found no significant incentive to provoke industrial relocation.

Yet to acquire 5,000 acres of industrial land, the TVA proposed flooding 2,000 acres of prime farmland. Overall, the plan called for the condemnation of 21,000 shoreline acres which the TVA would then sell at a $10.9 million profit to help finance the Tellico Dam. This meant the tax-exempt TVA was entering into direct competition with private property owners and land developers, a practice considered questionable even by pro-business *Nation's Business*.

Coalition disclosed that land losses TVA planners called "modest" included 10,000 acres of bottomland, yielding $3 million annually in agricultural production, and 15,600 acres of forest land valued at $58 million. In addition, the inundation would mean the loss of 156 forest jobs and nine years of genetic experimentation to breed superior trees.

The TVA claimed industry would be drawn by a navigable waterway, for which they counted $400,000 in yearly benefits. At present, the area produces no known commodity suitable for barge traffic, while two nearby waterways, Fort Loudon and Watts Bar, already provide thirteen major barge sites, largely unused. These two waterways have attracted only one small barge-using manufacturer in more than twenty years, hardly encouraging to Tellico backers.

It was claimed that annual benefits of over $500,000 would accrue to providing flood control. Yet this is supposedly a "flood-free" river; and furthermore, the Tellico Dam proposes to prevent downstream flooding by adding a mere .8 percent to the total storage of existing TVA reservoirs. It is unrealistic, the Coalition concluded, to assume the slight storage increase would have any real effect downstream.

When the Coalition had discredited all the other "benefits," they turned to "recreation," the largest, at $1.4 million a year. The length of the Little T already accommodates seven major dams, each of which includes recreational benefits in its own tally. In addition, twenty-two reservoirs lie within a fifty-mile radius, providing more than ample reservoir recreation. Tennessee's warm-water fish, the only fish the project could sustain, are now 80 percent unharvested. The Tellico project would only heighten the waste. The Coalition could find no justification for "benefits" here, especially considering the environment cost.

Importantly, the fact-finding included alternatives that would economically enhance the area without destroying it. Suggestions included developing the Little T as a recreation stream. Its unique opportunities for canoeing, fishing, archaeology, and so on support the Coalition's conclusion that millions of dollars would be attracted in private developments, docks, motels, and other tourist-related facilities. Judging from the examples of other states, the results would more than equal the purported benefits of the Tellico Project. The river's accessibility to the existing TVA vacation complex, Great Smoky Mountains National Park, and Cherokee National Forest, make the Little T a natural complement to the recreation of the whole region.

Facts and alternatives have proved an unbeatable match, at least so far. Halting the project, even temporarily, decreases its chances of success for two reasons. First, rising costs due to inflation reduce the benefit:cost ratio nearly every month. And second, the taste of success gives a dedicated group like the opponents of the Tellico Project the momentum necessary to push for a final victory.

3. *know the law*

No DISCUSSION OF environmental warfare is complete without at least a brief look at the arsenal of laws. Although some, like the Mining Act of 1872, sanction destruction, most laws would prevent it, if only they were strictly enforced. Legal steps may be taken at any point in the battle. It is important, however, to remember that they are more effective at halting authorization than construction. This is due simply to the fact that it is easier to stop a project when it is still in the planning stage.

Unfortunately, many of the projects now under fire were authorized as many as forty years ago when environmental allies were not as strong as they are today. Procedurally, an authorized bill may wait for years for appropriations. Unfunded is also unbuilt. If conservationists can create enough pressure to prevent a project's appropriation, they have eliminated the project. It is suggested that congressional pressure—that is, letter-writing campaigns, telegrams, and phone calls (all of which are carefully noted by any officials who depend on public election)—be exerted where it has the greatest likelihood of success.

Ordinarily, successful counterattack begins at the public hearing. Directives for the Corps of Engineers, the Bureau of Reclamation, and many other dam-builders stipulate that public hearings must be held several times during the planning process. Each hearing provides a chance for environmentalists to raise objections that will be duly recorded to accompany the proposal to Congress. The trouble is that notices for the hearings are often buried in the back pages of local papers, so meetings are poorly attended, and valid objections miss being put on the record. Only diligence and watchfulness prevent a project from rolling along unnoticed.

In some cases, the agency itself may provide a listing of projects it is considering. The Colorado Council of Trout Unlimited procured such a statewide listing from the BuRec and the Corps. They found no fewer than 204 projects, excluding those by private companies or municipalities, in one or another stage of planning or construction. Once the Council recovered from initial hysteria, it assigned project studies to TU chapters throughout the state. Each chapter dug into the vital data on the projects affecting its own area and particularly noted the project's stage of development: selling, planning, authorization, appropriation, or construction. In this way, the chapters and Council were able to assign priorities to each project according to the probability of success.

The National Environmental Policy Act

The law regarded by seasoned veterans of environmental battles as the most promising is the National Environmental Policy Act of 1970. It requires not only that project builders make an "Impact Statement," accounting for damages which would result from the proposed construction, but also that they consider alternatives to the project in depth. This shifts the burden of proof from the conservationists to the developers. Unfortunately, the impact study is not made by an impartial third party, so it is rarely a completely truthful, unbiased appraisal. But environmentalists are given a chance to amend, add, and correct the draft statement at a public review. A revised impact statement, containing both agency and public views, is then submitted to Congress, along with the feasibility study, for authorization.

If the agency has failed to make a complete impact statement, if they have made it inaccurately, or if public views have been slighted, the agency can be legally prevented from proceeding to Congress. Until the agency complies with a thorough environmental investigation, then, all agency progress halts pending revision of the impact statement.

This delaying tactic always works in favor of the conservationists by making a project increasingly difficult to justify. Costs rise over time, and the project's benefit:cost ratio falls. As its feasibility drops, so does its chance of success. Furthermore, the delay gives conservationists time to gather additional information, build public opinion and pressure, and possibly enact alternative legislation.

The case of the Cross-Florida Barge Canal should give hope to even the most timorous conservationist that a project not only authorized and funded but even partially constructed can be halted. The project was originally proposed in the 1880s to protect shipping from pirates. By the time construction finally began in the 1960s, the only pirates were the ones the Disney organization was recruiting for its nearby Walt Disney World. Of course, more cogent reasons replaced the pirate rationale, but the plans remained essentially the same. By the time the Environmental Policy Act was passed, the project had already been authorized and funded. Nonetheless, the Army Corps of Engineers was required to submit an Environmental Impact Statement.

Until this time, local residents had waged what appeared to be a fruitless fight. Finally, on the basis of the Corps' incomplete impact statement, they were able to secure a temporary injunction halting construction, already one third finished, until a more accurate impact statement could be filed. Before the final statement was made, President Nixon stepped in with an edict that halted the flagrantly illegal project. The Corps offered its standard argument that money would be wasted if the project were not completed and that some of the ditches were already dug. The President replied with an order to fill them in.

On the other side of the nation, a variation of the delay tactic is being used successfully to save the Middle Snake River, flowing free through Hell's Canyon, the deepest gorge in the country. Proposed projects to dam the Middle Snake anticipated the river would go the way of the Columbia and Lower Snake. But the Northwest Steelheaders, a group of dedicated fishermen now affiliated with Trout Unlimited, threw a wrench into the status quo. They were responsible for bringing to light the problem of nitrogen supersturation. Although they have not yet been able to halt construction of the last dam on the Lower Snake, they did succeed in preventing construction of the Asotin Dam, the first in a series planned for the Middle Snake.

Shortly thereafter, Congress issued a seven-year moratorium on any dam-building or construction on the river. The moratorium gives conservationists time to build Congressional support for a bill that will make the Middle Snake a National River and thereby preserve it in its present state forever.

The Clean Water Quality Act

Two additional laws have proven themselves particularly applicable for environmentalists. One, the Clean Water Quality Act of

1968, which forces stream classification according to purity, precipitated the cleanup of the South Platte River. The other, the Pelly Bill of 1971, enabled one man, Richard Buck, to save the North Atlantic salmon by empowering the President to place embargoes on the fish products of any nation whose fishing procedures threaten our fishery conservation program.

When the Cutthroat Chapter of Trout Unlimited in Littleton, Colorado, sallied forth to clean up the South Platte, the river had been polluted and without fish for some thirty-five years. Its low classification under the Clean Water Quality Act of 1968 kept it that way. But by providing for river classification, the law also provides the mechanism to upgrade the classification. This is where the TU chapter struck.

The impetus came from the chapter's program to educate the underprivileged youth of Denver in the fine art of trout fishing. Outfitted with renovated and donated tackle, the children would have no place to practice their newfound skill. The Platte, their most accessible fishing spot, not only had no fish but had even become unsafe for bodily contact.

The chapter decided to clean up the river, and the logical place to start was with reclassification. They petitioned the Water Pollution Control Commission, which would hear the case, to set a hearing date. Knowing that the Commission expected to hear only from irate conservationists, the chapter took a different tack. They began a quiet public education program, so that by the hearing date they had the support of everyone from the Junior League to various ghetto action groups.

Student supporters from the University of Denver made arrangements with the chapter to hire buses and bring additional battalions to the meeting. Television news teams followed close behind. When the local president of Trout Unlimited went to the podium to make his presentation and request, no fewer than seventy-two organizations' representatives followed him. In the face of such opposition the Commission could only rule in favor of reclassification, after which one commissioner was heard to remark to the chapter head, "You guys sure sandbagged us!"

With the new classification, the Cutthroat Chapter was able to proceed in securing aid to clean up the river and stock it with fish. Denver's eyesore and health hazard has again become a productive river. Next spring, there will be trout for young Waltons to take from the South Platte.

The Pelly Bill

For years the North Atlantic salmon fought an upstream battle against high Canadian inshore nettings and water pollution, until, by the early sixties, its very survival was threatened. Enlightened habitat restoration and hatchery programs began to bring back the majestic fish. The United States and Canada spent millions to protect the salmon from extinction. Norway, England, Ireland, Scotland, Greenland, and Iceland matched it with funds and programs of their own. By the mid-sixties, salmon were making a comeback. Maine had restored five major rivers, and four New England states were cooperating to bring back the salmon productivity of the Connecticut and Merrimack rivers.

Then a tragic discovery threatened to destroy everything they had accomplished. Until that time, part of the beautiful mystery of these salmon was that no one knew exactly where the mature fish went when they finished their downstream migration. In 1964, an ocean feeding ground was discovered in the Davis Strait, off the western coast of Greenland.

With no salmon-producing rivers of its own, Denmark took to the high seas to intercept the migrant fish. They spread efficient nylon nets as long as eighteen miles in length, each one with a 30-ton capacity. The catch was terrific. From about 36 metric tons in 1965, it leaped to more than 1,000 metric tons in 1969. The increased tonnage also included a disproportionately large number of fish. Catching salmon on the high seas means taking them before they reach even half their fully mature weight. Instead of 20-pounders, the Danes' catch was mostly seven-pound salmon—and 300,000 sea birds (not counted in the weight) that got tangled in the nets.

Naturally it wasn't long before the North Atlantic countries with salmon-producing rivers noted the tragic effect. The Atlantic catch on the Canadian shore alone decreased 47 percent in sports catches, 38 percent in commercial catches. In June, 1969, the fourteen-country International Commission for Northwest Atlantic Fisheries voted 11 to 2 (Denmark and West Germany), with one abstention, to ban all high seas fishing for the Atlantic salmon. Less than unanimous agreement, however, was not binding, and Denmark continued its netting. What the Danes considered their right to fish the high seas amounted to their right to destroy the fisheries of other nations.

Richard Buck, Vice-President of Trout Unlimited, devised a plan to weld together those organizations and individuals who should be concerned over the plight of the North Atlantic salmon into some sort of effective coalition. CASE, Committee on the Atlantic Salmon Emergency, was formed. Trout Unlimited approved CASE as an official project, and the International Atlantic Salmon Foundation underwrote a public information program for the first half of 1970.

With backing secured, one of the first things Buck did was bring together interested parties from most of the salmon-producing and fishing nations of the world. At the meeting, fishing experts and diplomats briefed them on the problem and on CASE's plans for action. Among its plans was the possibility of a boycott of all Danish goods. Until definitive action could be taken on the boycott, CASE concentrated on publicizing the predicament of the salmon.

In June, 1970, the International Commission for Northwest Atlantic Fisheries voted again. This time they secured an agreement from the Danish government to hold their catch to 1969 levels. Not encouraging for the future of the salmon, the agreement at least represented the first restrictions on the taking of Atlantic salmon on the high seas. CASE moved into Phase II, the evolution of a program which would put pressure on the Danish government by rousing into action the American public's traditional sense of fair play.

Newspapers, radio, and television carried stories of the tragedy of the salmon. By fall, the office of the Danish Ambassador was swamped by an ever-increasing volume of outraged mail. Senators and congressmen began to feel the pressure for action. CASE swung into high gear.

It held a "Save our Salmon" dinner, attended by TU directors Bing Crosby and Curt Gowdy and other internationally known fishermen. Danish television cameras were there when Ted Williams and others explained their personal boycotts of Danish goods. The Danish public heard the facts about what high seas salmon fishing meant to the rest of the world: the immediate economic loss to commercial and sports catches and the long chain of secondary effects on research and hatcheries, sportsmen's travel, lodgings, and license expenses.

As a result, CASE was invited to Copenhagen to lay its concerns before government agencies and the Danish people. In response, the government made another halfhearted concession. This time, they agreed to reduce the number of boats from seventeen to fourteen. Meanwhile, in the United States, pressure continued to mount. With other avenues closed, Washington took the steps necessary to exert economic sanctions. Congress introduced the Pelly Bill, and Mr. Buck and his committee returned to Washington to testify in favor of the legislation.

In the fall of 1971, the Pelly Bill was passed. The clout it gave the President succeeded in forcing the Danes to phase out all high seas fishing over the next four years. The salmon catch will return to the pre-Davis-Strait discovery level, and, with ongoing conscientious water management, salmon will continue to swim in the waters of the North Atlantic rim. Children will know the electric thrill of the tug of a fresh-run salmon against a sporting tackle. The more than 100,000 breadwinners who depend on the fish for their livelihood will not have to seek other jobs, and one more precious recreational resource will be preserved—all because one man, Richard Buck, had the dedication and drive to alert an entire country to save this monarch of the world of sport fish for generations to come.

4. *know the alternatives*

B Y NOW IT must be clear that there is an alternative to environmental destruction. Disastrous projects can be halted, new and better management substituted for bad, fouled streams renewed, and endangered species protected. It is equally true that alternatives exist within the conservationist camp. When one road goes nowhere, another may lead to success. Hundreds of fishing streams and rivers across the country bear witness to the ingenuity of the concerned citizens who set about to protect them.

Knowing the alternatives gives environmentalists the flexibility to change directions and still win the fight. If a dam isolates one spawning ground, technology may create new ones. If a stream will not support sensitive rainbows, it may sustain a sturdier trout. If hatchery fish provide no challenge to sports fishermen, supplemental stream feeding may grow wild trout more efficiently. The alternatives are endless, but the future of fisheries depends on the adaptibility and vision of the conservationists to apply them.

Northwestern Activities

In the Northwest, where dams and pollution have decimated the great runs of salmon and steelhead and conservationists battle to prevent additional destruction, enlightened fisheries management presents a productive alternative. Federal fisheries agencies assist state agencies in Washington, Oregon, California, and Idaho to restore the fish runs.

Genetic research has developed disease-resistant species and strains of rapid-growth fish, like the Donaldson Rainbow. Super-efficient hatcheries built below the lowest dam are producing fantastic quantities of trout, salmon, and steelhead for the new spawning grounds they have created. By removing natural obstacles from the waterways still open to the sea and imprinting the fish with chemical characteristics of those streams, biologists ensure the trout's unerring return once it has been released to find the sea. When the anadromous fish return to spawn, they are recaptured and manually spawned to continue the cycle. Salmon and steelhead have adapted well to the new procedures, proving readily manageable in this manner.

In the State of Washington, hatchery programs actually proved overly successful; they turned out more silver salmon than they had manpower or equipment to distribute to the available streams. The Fish and Game Department enlisted the help of the Northwest Steelheaders Council of Trout Unlimited. The TU "Steelheaders" and Department personnel loaded the young salmon in fifty-five-gallon drums which they stacked on the chapter's boat trailers. Members then distributed the fish to barren but biologically suitable streams in the state. Formerly fishless waters now host healthy silver salmon. Surrounding states and British Columbia are investigating the possibility of adapting this "Barren Rivers Program" to renew some of their own nonproductive streams.

The Au Sable Syndrome

The French called the river "Au Sable," River of Sand. Michigan calls it one of the state's finest trout streams for the same reason. About three quarters of the 2,000-mile area the river drains is sandy. As a result the river remains relatively stable the year round, rising only moderately in the springtime. Even after the fishing season, the Au Sable averages 777 trout per acre. But the Au Sable has the same problems as other rivers: It is dammed and diverted and polluted. That it is also a superb trout stream is due to the systematic use of alternatives by fishery managers.

When great pine forests lined the upland riverbanks, the fish were as prevalent as they are now. The fish was grayling, and it drew fishermen from as far away as Norway, Sweden, and the British Isles, where indigenous graylings delighted generations of anglers. Trains and wagons brought fishermen by the thousands. Although the fine game fish was easy prey for all who wished to catch him in a sporting manner, he would never have disappeared if railroad loggers had not stripped the riverbanks of their pines.

By 1892, the forest was gone. Stream-bed logs were removed, and overhanging sweepers also disappeared to accommodate river traffic. The Au Sable silted up and became too warm to support the frail grayling, which was chased from one Michigan river to another until it disappeared entirely from the state's river system. Native brook trout followed.

Rather than allow their river to die, fishery managers imported rainbows from the Pacific Cascades to stock the river. Once again the Au Sable became a famed fishery, this time for the western import. Soon six hydroelectric dams were built across the main stem of the river. Poor land management, pollution from the mills, and the damming of the river warmed and dirtied the water until the rainbows too were unable to survive.

The managers stepped in again, with the hardy brown or Lock Leven trout from Europe. Although the browns were more adaptable than their native North American cousins, they too were bound to disappear unless effective conservation measures cleaned up the Au Sable. Today, the river survives as a great brown trout fishery, and choice native brook trout are returning in greater and greater numbers.

The William B. Mershon Chapter of Trout Unlimited in Saginaw has been subtly improving eleven miles of the South Branch of the Au Sable by providing trout cover for the flies-only portion of the stream. In 1955, George Mason, co-founder of the chapter, gave 1,500 acres to the state for a game preserve, providing no live trees were ever cut from the area. The old stumps and logs that create new hiding spots for trout are made of dead materials from the nearby woods. The logs, wired to posts set out of the main stream to avoid interfering with canoeists, provide protective hideouts for the trout during low water. Even the naturally suspicious fish don't recognize the structures as artificial and can be seen moving among the logs within two hours of their placement, so it is a cinch fishermen can't recognize the man-made improvements. All the same, the success of the Au Sable derives from the imaginative management that has prevailed for over a century.

The Great Lakes

Enlightened and aggressive fishery policies have saved other waterways according to the Au Sable example of consecutive alternatives. Among these, the Great Lakes is a classic. Before the days of the canals and the St. Lawrence Seaway, the lakes produced lake trout, walleyed pike, bass, and other native species. When the canals first opened, they brought prosperity to towns along their courses—and the lamprey eel to the lake waters. The eel, a parasite which feeds on live fish, found the Great Lakes trout so much to its liking that within twenty years it had brought one of the greatest fisheries in the country to virtual extinction.

The Great Lakes states and the United States Bureau of Sport Fisheries and Wildlife, working together, developed a lampricide that worked successfully in the biological system of the Great Lakes. At the same time, plankton-eating alewives multiplied in the Great Lakes in such vast numbers that massive die-offs closed the beaches. They discovered that large areas within the lakes were fishless, a fact they put to good use once the lamprey control program began to take effect. Howard Tanner and Wayne Tody of the Michigan Department of Natural Resources recommended planting Pacific salmon in these fishless areas. Since the lamprey no longer threatened the fish, the salmon could feed on the alewives and would not compete with the warm-water fishery along the shore.

Chinook and coho salmon were introduced into the lakes. Steelhead recovered, and lake-run brown trout returned to the waters. Not only did the Michigan Department of Natural Resources stave off the extinction of fish but in some instances it actually increased their numbers. The rebirth of the Great Lakes as a fishery is due to creative management and to the use of alternatives.

Artificial versus Real Trout

Colorado, like any other state which features full-color photos of successful anglers in its tourist brochures, poses a problem for its fisheries management. Each year, ever-increasing numbers of fishermen come to Colorado to fish in less and less water. Native trout can not endure the increased trade without help from a hatchery program. Unfortunately, as the demand for catchable trout grows, fishery policy becomes increasingly one-sided. To supply catchable trout, budgets are weighted in favor of hatchery programs, and money is pirated from long-range management protection and stream restoration.

In 1970, 73 percent of the entire fisheries budget in Colorado went into the production of hatchery trout to plant in front of the rods of tourist fishermen. The demand, in essence, is for dead fish. Of course, dead fish can not reproduce themselves, and streams are kept from becoming self-sustaining. As a result, hatchery costs continue their upward spiral.

Fish grown to maturity in hatcheries are unused to the wilds. To them, an arm swinging out over the water means food, not danger. For the state, however, it means tourist trade. The wily, naturally produced trout provide a far greater challenge to the sports fisherman. Inexperienced tourists, unable to meet the challenge of the native trout, will almost certainly never return to the same stream. Officials fear he may not return to the state.

A recent study in Montana proves that the massive infusion of hatchery fish into a river that supports a substantial wild trout population is detrimental to both. The wild trout will win the struggle for food and space, but fall spawning and the rigorous winter find them in a decidedly weakened condition. Colorado Trout Unlimited demanded to know the facts about artificial and naturally produced trout statewide. During the fall, when the water level is low, the state's twenty-two fisheries biologists could have easily tallied the trout. In 1969, they were manning big game stations counting elk and deer. The following year, TU got its survey. In the spring and summer, hatchery programs poured hundreds of thousands of catchable trout into Colorado rivers. By fall, only 3 to 4 percent of the remaining population were artificially produced rainbows. The remainder was the unaided, unstocked brown trout.

If Colorado and other states would emphasize the wild character of the fisheries, they would succeed in promoting sports fishing at far lower cost. Fingerling or subyearling stocking produces stronger, more sporting (and better-tasting) trout than traditional put-and-take stocking methods. With adequate trout protection and habitat and water quality improvements, stocking may even become unnecessary for all but the streams incapable of producing their own populations of fish.

In North Carolina, a group of individuals took over a small private stream. Unable to afford stocking the water, they tried supplemental stream feeding, introducing a commercial trout chow two to three times a week at five points along the stream. Before supplemental feeding, the capture of a 13-inch trout was cause for an all-night celebration. Within approximately five years, there was a tremendous increase in the pounds-per-acre of trout, and catching 18- to 22-inch trout in fighting trim became such a regular occurrence that celebration was reserved for the over-25-inchers.

Trout Unlimited is convinced that it is far more feasible in some instances to grow fish in streams than in expensive hatcheries which have a built-in transportation expense. Nonethelesss, TU has been unable to convince one fish and game department to undertake even a joint research project. So until private research proves methods like supplemental stream feeding applicable to a large-scale operation, only small private streams will produce fighting wild trout through this method for limited numbers of fishermen.

5. *develop* a Schtick

An entertainer learns early in his career the importance of a gimmick to set his particular talent apart from all the rest. The skillful craftsman will then use this *schtick* to point up to what he is saying or doing. In much the same way, against all the other visual and mental and emotional stimuli that attract people of our modern age, the environmentalist must compete for public attention. There must be something catchy about his message; otherwise it will be lost among the many that are heard each day: "Buy this," "Save that," "Do something else." The environmentalist must develop a *schtick* with gusto enough to make his demands louder and clearer than the others.

Yo-yos and Signs

In the interest of variety, perhaps, there is no one rule for developing an effective *schtick*. It varies from battle to battle. Take the case of fluctuating water levels in slack-water reservoirs. Two groups attacked the problem in entirely different ways. But each employed a *gimmick*.

Art Flick, a fly tier and excellent sports fisherman, was accustomed to fine fishing in New York State's Catskills. The disappointing catches which resulted from the varying water levels on the New York Water Supply reservoirs frustrated Flick to action. He bought all the yo-yos he could find and mailed them to the Army Corps of Engineers to protest the up-and-down fluctuations of its reservoirs. Other members of the Catskill Mountain Chapter of TU and their friends took up the practice. Soon thousands of yo-yos arrived at the Corps office. Realizing the severity of the public's displeasure with its reservoir policies, the Corps re-examined its management.

The Chattahoochee Chapter in Atlanta faced the same problem. When they demanded a safe and stable river flow from their local reservoir project, the Army Corps of Engineers, once again the offending agency, rebuffed their every appeal. In desperation they posted signs all along the river.

This river subject to sudden and violent water changes without warning. These changes are controlled by the United States Army Corps of Engineers at Buford Dam. Despite several requests by concerned citizens, the Army Corps of Engineers has refused to install an audible alarm system or make their schedule available to the public. If you share our concern with regard to this threat to human life, we suggest you write your Congressman or contact us.

Trout Unlimited

Replies came fast and furious. Within a few months, the Corps was sufficiently embarrassed to comply with chapter demands for some sort of warning system. Another poster campaign succeeded in Aspen, Colorado. The Ferdinand-Hayden Chapter of Trout Unlimited watched improperly treated sewage pour into their Roaring Fork River. The well-traveled route of hearings and petitions to the Health Department got nowhere. A new sewage treatment plant was planned for the future that would alleviate some of the pollution of the Roaring Fork. But four years was too long to wait; by then, the Roaring Fork would be destroyed forever.

Signs reading *Fish taken from the Roaring Fork unfit for human consumption* turned up all along the river. Soon notices appeared in all their frank splendor in Rocky Mountain newspapers. Local media carried the story. In no time at all, Aspen's new sewage plant was in full operation, well ahead of schedule.

TV Time

The Cutthroat Chapter in Denver, which succeeded in forcing reclassification of the South Platte, found the Army Corps of Engineers had major plans for channeling the river they had worked so hard to save. Upstream, the Corps was building the Chatfield Dam for purposes of flood control. Yet flood control was the reason given for channeling the South Platte.

The dam provides a guaranteed cold-water flow to the South Platte by drawing from the deepest water of the reservoir. While TU favored the dam, it could not endorse channeling the river. The chapter organized again all the conservation groups and social agencies that helped them in the reclassification drive. When the coalition realized that the Corps' plans would render all their efforts for naught, they drafted resolutions censuring the project. Newspaper articles were written, and the regional director of the Corps of Engineers was challenged to a televised debate with conservationists.

With the weight of evidence clearly on the side of the conservationists, the Corps of Engineers was at a decided disadvantage. As a result of the television debacle, newspaper coverage, and an aroused populace, the director recommended the project be withdrawn for further study.

TU and its allies developed an alternative plan: converting upstream riverside properties into a flood-plain park, thereby making channeling downstream unnecessary. In order to realize these plans for the flood plain, the coalition needed to pass bond issues to finance the project in the three cities upstream from Denver. Littleton, the farthest upstream and the least prosperous of the three, was the first to vote in favor of the bond issue. Englewood and Sheridan, the remaining cities, will almost certainly follow Littleton's lead. When the Corps presents its revised plans for the South Platte, they will have to be in keeping with TU demands, demands which have been reflected in the preference of other Denver citizen groups and at the voting booths of three upstream cities.

The Unmentioned Slough Line

The Lower Granite Dam mentioned in Chapter 1 was originally the concern only of the Army Corps of Engineers and the "Steelheaders" of the Inland Empire Chapter of Trout Unlimited in Spokane. The latter were particularly imaginative in bringing their case to the people. Although the suits are still unresolved, they would never have been initiated if this Washington chapter hadn't aroused the public. The Corps would have kept on digging, and the fish would have kept on dying. Now at least the Corps is making some attempts to rectify the problems caused by its unrestrained and unnecessary dam-building.

The alert vice-president of this chapter was in nearby Lewiston, Idaho, the same time the Corps made its pitch to the local Chamber of Commerce at the town's most fashionable country club. The club occupies an elevated spot above the Snake River, and its shoreline golf course rolls away toward the water's edge. The TU member decided a dramatic demonstration was needed to thwart the Corps' plans for passive receptivity.

He drove up to the golf course, removed from his truck heavy wooden stakes tied with red flags, and began hammering the stakes at intervals along a straight line running through fairways, sand traps, and greens. It wasn't long before a club member hurried over to demand an explanation. With a hearty grin and an all-American handshake, the TU member identified himself as "Mr. Johnson of the Corps of Engineers." He was assigned, he explained, to mark the eventual slough line, beyond which the ground would slip downward once the dam had filled and its waters backed upriver. His listener blanched and, hurrying off to report his findings, disappeared inside the clubhouse.

When the country club learned that the Corps had indeed neglected to mention its concern over the dam's eventual slough line and that it would be necessary to dike the area near the club to protect the golf course, TU won over a whole cadre of staunch supporters.

The Selling Package

In order to convince the general public that forestry practices on the Umpqua River were destroying the forest, the Umpqua steamboaters put together a program featuring all the destruction of the Umpqua.

Accustomed to the business of "selling a package," two San Francisco ad men who belong to TU made a movie, *Pass Creek,* portraying the effects of poor forestry management in the watershed, especially on the headwaters and feeder streams of the Umpqua. Shot entirely by amateurs, *Pass Creek* was made for approximately $5,000, an incredibly low budget for a film of this type. It was aired on public television, at forestry schools and clubs across the nation, and finally in the United States Congress. The movie is still available on request from Trout Unlimited.

Since most visitors to the forest never saw the carefully concealed instances of abuse, the "Madmen of Montana" devised their own tour. This one highlighted clear-cut, eroded hillsides and devastated streams. Besides a professional dissertation on proper forestry practices, the program included a briefing on relevant laws and an afternoon hike to where the devastation spoke most plainly. The grand finale was a flight over the damaged area in small private planes. Congressmen, senators, conservationists, industrialists, and park visitors took the special tour. As pressure built, more and more people came to the forest to see the damage.

The mounting pressure engendered by the tour forced the detailed investigation into the management policies of the Bitterroot described in Chapter 2. When the facts laid bare the full extent of the depredation, a new management system was initiated for the Bitterroot and other U.S. Forest Service holdings throughout the country.

6. cooperate

Cooperate is as important an imperative as any other in the "battle plan." The question "With whom?" is easily answered. Cooperate with any individual or organization that is willing to do so. This doesn't mean compromise; it does mean combine for action. With your goals firmly in mind, find others who are willing to work toward them with the same vigor and dedication.

Environmental veterans have learned not to be surprised at the sources of cooperation. It is not unusual to find that the enemies of one battle are the allies of the next. Such was the case of the Pacific Gas and Electric Company in California. The utility firm's power dam across Hat Creek backed up a portion of the river and resulted in its infestation by warm-water trash fish. The warm-water fish traveled upstream to free-flowing parts of the river, until very few of the remaining fish population were salmonoids.

The California Council of Trout Unlimited was critical of the state's fisheries priorities, which emphasized providing catchable trout at the expense of habitat improvement for existing wild trout. TU maintained that the public would prefer a fishery which offered wild trout regardless of protective low-kill limits. Pacific Gas and Electric agreed to cooperate with TU and the California Fish and Game Department to test the theory.

They built two fish barriers: one at the head of their lake, the other upstream to isolate a portion of the river. The State Fish and Game Department removed fish from the test portion of the river, and TU stocked it with the finest strains of wild fish on the West Coast. Catch and release became the rule on this portion of Hat Creek. Nonetheless, it proved far and away the most popular area of the river. In fact, the fishing public so obviously preferred wild trout that the Fish and Game Department is currently looking for twenty-two additional sites on which to initiate similar programs.

Another research project led the Michigan Department of Natural Resources to ask Trout Unlimited's cooperation in determining why steelhead trout preferred one small tributary to all the other rivers in a local river system. The tributary, Little Garlic River, appeared no different from other available spawning streams. Wags joked that perhaps the steelhead were a strain of Italian trout who preferred a Garlic River to any other. But because the river was on private land, the Department was not permitted to do the necessary research. It requested Trout Unlimited to buy the land and place it in the public domain. TU agreed, but on condition that, when the study was completed, the river would remain in its wild state and public access would be guaranteed.

The Department approved the arrangement, and a grant from TU's president purchased the tract. The study, now underway, will reveal valuable information for improving fishery management statewide and nationally.

Help from Industry

With the recent surge of interest in the ecology, industry too has shown itself willing to work with conservationists to solve problems to mutual satisfaction. Willard Rockwell, Chairman of the Board of North American Rockwell, is a national director of Trout Unlimited. With his own corporation at the forefront of environmental protection, Rockwell recommended to the Nixon Administration an environmental program that applied industrial management techniques to national conservation. Eastman Kodak installed a $6.5 million industrial waste purification plant and adopted "Terry the Trout," swimming in the treated waste water, as the symbol of its effectiveness. Timber, pulp, and paper firms, like Georgia Pacific, Pope and Talbott, and Boise Cascade, worked with Trout Unlimited to establish logging practices that would safeguard the watersheds and protect wildlife habitat.

In May, 1970, while attending a conference which hosted members of industry and conservation organizations, the Executive Director of Trout Unlimited received an urgent call from one of his Washington chapters. The chapter reported that Boise Cascade, one of the firms attending the conference, was destructively logging over a small tributary which flows into a river supporting major runs of steelhead and sea-run cutthroat in southwestern Washington. When the general meetings concluded, the Executive Director arranged a private discussion with the Boise representative for later that evening.

As a result of their meeting, a Boise vice-president was in southwestern Washington within a week to review the problem with his own timber manager and a representative from Trout Unlimited. When the State of Washington fined the timber giant, Boise not only unquestioningly paid the fine but cleared the stream of logging debris. The firm then established an ongoing relationship with the local Trout Unlimited chapter to prevent a recurrence.

Industries may well be expected to "clean up after themselves." The fact that they have neglected to do this for so many years makes cooperation such as Boise Cascade's notable. But sometimes industrial cooperation extends far beyond ordinary parameters. In Aspen, Colorado, another of TU's national directors, Philip Wright, made a habit of carrying home a full creel of paper, empty beer cans, and miscellaneous debris he found on the waters he fished. As the idea caught on among local fishermen, Wright decided to expand it with creels especially designed to serve as litter bags. Potato sacks would be perfect. Inexpensive, biodegradable yet durable, and large, they could be imprinted with an antilitter message on one side and the industrial sponsor's message on the other. With a sample reading "Creel Your Litter—Not Your Limit," TU set out to find their first sponsor.

Wally Haas, president of Levi Strauss, assumed the role, producing thousands of creels to be freely distributed. Strauss creels can now be seen all over the country, and other sponsors have stepped forward. Store windows in cities throughout the country feature a litter creel stuffed with debris and bearing the query, "Have you caught your limit lately?"

The Colorado Open Space Coordinating Council

Colorado, which seemed to pioneer cooperation between industry and conservation groups, also introduced a coordinating council to promote cooperation among conservation organizations. In the mid-1960s, six conservation organizations, frustrated by the denial of representation in the legislature, formed the Colorado Open Space Coordinating Council. Now COSCC represents forty-two organizations, each with one vote on the board. Any one of the member organizations may bring an issue before the Council. If a simple majority agrees to take on the project, COSCC will bring the issue to the public and, through them, to the legislature.

The Colorado Open Space Coordinating Council has worked so effectively that it has been adopted as a model for state and regional coordinating councils across the country. At the national level, the National Resources Council of America utilizes its *modus operandi*. Rather than function politically, the National Resources Council serves as a forum to coordinate far-flung organizations which maintain representatives in Washington, D.C. The increasing effectiveness of the conservation movement is due largely to their success in mobilizing divergent organizations to focus on a particular issue.

Gold-Medal Gray's Run

What began as an effort to preserve a small cold stream flowing through the mountains of Lycoming County, Pennsylvania, became a three-year project to preserve and protect the entire Gray's Run Watershed. Forty years ago, the Civilian Conservation Crops built forty-five log dams on the Gray's Run River in north-central Pennsylvania. Over the years, many of the dams deteriorated and were washed away by spring runoffs. Logs, combined with fallen trees and other debris, clogged some of the river's deep pools. The Susquehanna Chapter of Trout Unlimited saw the opportunity to restore the Gray's Run and teach young people a lesson in conservation.

Dwaine E. Gipe, member of TU, was also executive of the West Branch Council of the Boy Scouts. He coordinated the project, which finally involved more than a thousand men and boys. First biologists from the Pennsylvania Fish Commission and the United States Fish and Wildlife Service surveyed the area and detailed the plans for restoration. Special summer work days were scheduled. More than 45,000 man hours were spent installing channel blocks to keep the stream in its main channel, removing debris that interfered with stream flow, reinforcing the embankment to prevent erosion, and constructing devices that would concentrate current and water flow in the desired location. In areas where natural cover was necessary, the Scouts and the chapter created deep-water pools with log diverters.

Improving the stream resulted in its ability to support wild trout without periodic stocking of hatchery fish. The increase in the natural trout population has been tremendous. In some areas, as much as 100 percent improvement was noted. In addition to the actual stream improvement, game feeder stations were installed, forestry demonstration areas laid out, and nature trails built along most of the stream.

For their conservation efforts, the Boy Scouts won the 1968 Gold Seal Conservation Award, the highest award the United States Department of Agriculture can bestow on a private citizen or group for its contribution to conservation. The Scouts coupled their love of the outdoors with sound conservation principles. Besides restoring the Gray's Run, the project created a cadre of conservationists who will continue to respect and preserve natural resources through sound conservation principles.

Nix on Tocks

Cooperation among various agencies is important, but intra-agency cooperation is even more so. At the local level, it must occur among TU members; at state and regional levels, among all constituent parts. In northern New Jersey, during the summer of 1969, Trout Unlimited formed a small chapter in Sparta. At the same time, the Tocks Island Dam and Reservoir proposal, approved some seven years earlier, was brought up for a $250 million appropriation.

The project called for impounding the Delaware River above the famous Water Gap. This would back water thirty-five miles upstream to Port Jervis, New York, ostensibly to provide water power, flood control, and recreation. Numerous tributary trout streams in northern New Jersey and the Pocono Mountains of Pennsylvania would be flooded, along with farmlands and forest. The project was locally popular. Only a few recognized the environmental threat and the boondoggle. One of them hand-lettered a sign that appeared along the river: "No more shad, oysters, farms, forests. Eat an engineer for lunch tomorrow. Nix on Tocks."

Among those who shared that opinion were the forty members of the newly formed TU chapter, including professionals from the media, professors of economics, and biologists, all of whom believed that the project would die of its own deficiencies if it were exposed to clear public view. The chapter called upon the Washington office of TU to help them build their case. The New York and Pennsylvania councils lent their time and expertise. Soon the Sparta Chapter had put together a dossier of undeniable strength.

They set up speaking dates, worked with local newspapers and other media, contacted congressmen and state representatives, even interviewed the Governor. By summer, 1971, the chapter's efforts brought Russell Train, Chairman of the President's Council on Environmental Quality, to Tocks Island with an order to halt further work or expenditure, pending a complete environmental and economic review. Though the final verdict has not yet been made, cooperation through the national, state, and local level of one dedicated conservation group has enabled the organization to say "Nix on Tocks," at least so far.

7. conserve

POLLUTION IS LIKE an illness which ravages a body and leaves it unable to sustain life. With disease, when it is possible to choose between prevention and cure, a physician will axiomatically prefer the former. So do conservationists. Ergo the raging battles to halt unnecessary projects like the Tellico and Snake River dams.

It is unquestionably wiser to preserve natural resources than to try to recreate an ecosystem once it has been destroyed. The interdependence of the air, the plants, the insect life, the fish, and the water is so incredibly complex that undertaking their reconstruction automatically limits success to man's technological level. That is to say, all efforts to undo damage are doomed to at least some degree of failure.

Of the 2.3 .billion acres of land and water that were once wild America, only 10 percent remains truly unspoiled. Most of that is in Alaska, the last frontier. But Alaska is more than that; it is America's last chance to use its national heritage wisely. When despoiled waterways accuse this country of ignorance, avarice, and negligence at every turn, Alaska remains more than half a million square miles of pristine wilderness. Nowhere is the need for preventive conservation more manifest than here.

Yet with all the benefit of hindsight, man is applying his frontier philosophy of "use, abuse, and move on" to this last frontier. His waste of America's resources is proof positive that they are not truly inexhaustible. Still, too many regard Alaska as Henry Pratt does. The executive assistant to Alaska's former Governor Keith Miller maintained, "Hell, this country's so goddamn big that even if industry ran wild we could never wreck it" (quoted by Tom Brown in *Oil on Ice,* Sierra Club, 1971). Men like this, proven wrong eveywhere in the world, are already leaving scars on the state's trackless wilderness.

Alaska virtually mirrors continental America in every aspect of its development. When white men first came to Alaska, they found Indians, Aleuts, and Eskimos. Darker skinned than European Americans, the natives suffered much the same fate as their cousins in the rest of the Americas. In 1884, the United States Congress legally recognized that Alaskan natives had certain rights. The Alaskan Organic Act, passed in that year, left Congress with the authority to determine exactly what those rights would be. Congress has yet to get around to it. So with its potential riches of copper, coal, zinc, tin, and timber, to say nothing of its controversial oil reserves, Alaska is still one of the poorest states in the Union. One half of every dollar spent within Alaskan borders is Federal agency giveaway money. As might be expected, the natives suffer most from this state of servile dependency. Beyond the white man's initial gifts, tuberculosis and syphilis, they expect little and receive even less.

Only now is Congress wrestling with the problems posed almost a century ago. With the advent of statehood, Alaska was given until 1984 to complete its selection of any 103 million acres as state lands. As the time draws near, competition increases for the choicest tidbits. Understandably, native claims include the most desirable parts of Alaska, much of which is uninhabitable. But these areas are simultaneously critical to the continued existence of the fish and wildlife in the state. Now that oil has been discovered, confirming long-standing suspicions, the future of Alaska's environment becomes increasingly tenuous.

So poor so long, the natives view the proposed exploitation of oil resources as a boon. For them it means billions of dollars; to conservationists irrevocable destruction. Klondike Fever is just an indigenous manifestation of the greed that has preceded environmental destruction wherever it has occurred. As legal as native claims may be, the unplundered wilderness of Alaska belongs to all Americans. Natives must be compensated promptly and equitably, but the land must be utilized carefully on behalf of every citizen.

The Alaskan ecological balance is unquestionably the most frail in the country. Nearly one third of the state lies within the Arctic Circle. Extreme cold statewide results in growing seasons only two months long, and sometimes less. The delicate lichen-covered tundra consequently produces ground cover at a rate of one inch every fifty years. In the 1920s wagons rolled across Seward Peninsula twice. The tracks are clearly visible today. It is difficult to say how many centuries it will take to erase the ruts made by modern heavy machinery.

The fragile climate, which many label "hostile," manifests itself in the fisheries. Generally regarded as the finest cold-water fisheries in the world, Alaskan rivers and bays have a notoriously low productivity. In Bristol Bay, in Alaska's southwest, 10-pound rainbows are from eight to twelve years old. Farther north, the fish are even older.

The stability of the Alaskan ecosystem depends on its permafrost, permanently frozen subsoil. Some is gravel or rock, which thaws without environmental disturbance, but much is ice-rich silty soil, held in place by its frozen water content. Disturbing the thin layer of soil and ground-hugging vegetation that insulates the permafrost against thawing in the summer has incalculable consequences. The soil erodes and resettles, causing serious drainage and frost problems. Once upset, the equilibrium is destroyed and turns on itself in a spiral of destruction nearly impossible to reverse.

In 1968, Atlantic Richfield discovered an oil reserve of 5 to 10 billion barrels at Prudhoe Bay. Planes and barges brought other explorers and their heavy equipment to Alaska's North Slope by the hundreds, until former Governor Walter J. Hickel ordered a 400-mile road to improve logistics. Winter roads in the Arctic are usually made by packing snow on top of the tundra to form a raised path. In contrast, the Hickel Highway excavated a roadway through the permafrost. Completed in the winter of 1968–69, its major problem was snow removal. The following spring, however, the highway might well have been renamed Hickel Canal. The melted slush was impassable, and the road had to be rerouted the next winter. Learning nothing from the previous year's experience, road-builders left two slashes instead of one. Given Alaska's brief growing season, the scars will remain forever.

Oil exploration brought still more destruction. Behind every work camp is a cesspool into which pours all the waste water of the camp. Frozen in the winter months, the lagoon becomes a foul bog with the spring thaw. Even during these early periods of exploration, when human habitation was minimal, the resultant problems were severe enough to be labeled a health hazard by the Federal Water Quality Administration. The climate precludes constructing septic tanks or diluting sewage runoffs in free-flowing streams. Federal and state agencies are now working to establish guidelines to eliminate the sewage problem.

If they are successful, litter remains another unsolved dilemma. In an effort to counter criticism, Atlantic Richfield began a cleanup program in 1969. Drilling sites are now conspicuously immaculate. Previous invaders were not as careful. At the Naval Petroleum Reserve in Barrow, barrels of oil were left behind by departing contractors to rust in the snow. Some were full. When the army left Amchitka following World War II, thousands of Quonset huts, tons of trash, and useless airplane hulks were simply bulldozed off a convenient cliff. The cold climate has naturally retarded decomposition, and trash and metal parts still litter the hillside.

Now that oil is no longer a speculative resource, destruction is magnified a thousand times. It took two hundred years for America to destroy much of its continental heritage. Our technology now makes it possible to crush Alaska much quicker. Consider the proposed Trans-Alaskan Pipeline.

To carry an initial flow of 500,000 (eventually 2 million) barrels per day from the North Slope to the all-weather port of Valdez and recoup some of their $2 billion investment, the oil companies have proposed laying eight hundred miles of pipe across Alaska. All but fifty miles would be sunk four to ten feet into the permafrost. This bedrock of Alaskan environmental stability is likely to become "permaslush." Oil pours from the ground at a temperature of 140 degrees, and twelve pumping stations along the route should keep it that temperature for most of its journey.

The proposed pipeline would pass over no less than twenty-four rivers, hundreds of streams, and dozens of lakes. On the Yukon River alone, native Alaskans catch 450,000 fish per year. The Alaskan Fish and Game Department reports there is no place along the line where an important watershed would not be threatened by a major spill.

Spills are a virtual certainty, inasmuch as two thirds of the pipeline would run through Alaska's "Ring of Fire," an earthquake zone which has registered twenty-three quakes of Richter 6 or better since 1901. Before retiring as Secretary of the Interior, Walter Hickel reported to the Chairman of the Senate's Interior Committee, "We can not provide assurance that large earthquakes will not rupture the pipeline."

To minimize the destruction of an oil spill (which is to minimize a total disaster), shutoff valves would be situated approximately every sixty miles. Each mile of pipe, however, would contain 500,000 gallons of oil, twice the amount that gummed up Santa Barbara in 1969. When the oil reached its destination at Valdez, it would be loaded into supertankers twice the size of those in operation today and carried to Seattle, Portland, and San Francisco along one of the most treacherous shipping lanes in the world. The waters the tankers intend to ply are considered by many to represent the most critically important fish habitats to be found anywhere. An accident here would unquestionably mean disaster.

At the port of Valdez, a continental shelf keeps the giant tankers thirty miles offshore. A terminal here would be exposed to violent arctic storms which sometimes rage for days. In these cold waters, any spill wouldn't disperse or decompose for centuries.

Although fully aware of the imminence of oil spills, Secretary of the Interior Rogers Morton drafted an Environmental Impact Statement that assumed the pipeline posed no significant threat to the environment. The statement failed to provide any compensation for losses incurred from the pipeline, either as a result of construction that would relocate natives who make their living along the proposed route or in case of spill.

When this statement was made, the Alyeska Pipeline Company, a subsidiary of seven oil companies that would build the pipe, had not yet formulated its design. Representatives explained to a Washington hearing that they would build it "as we go along." What they were proposing, in essence, was that given the chance to transport the black gold across Alaska, they would do their best; if something went wrong, they would be sorry. Hardly justified in a temperate climate, this rationale is inexcusable in Alaska.

The Draft Impact Statement compounded its faults by assuming without proof that development of Alaskan oil reserves is essential to national security. The Department of the Interior projects America's need for oil will reach 20 million barrels per day by 1980. By then, this country will only produce about 13.3 million barrels daily. Imported oil would make up the difference, with 20 percent of that coming from the volatile Middle East.

What appears at first glance a bona fide crisis is strictly man-made. At present America's domestic oil production is held to artificially low levels to keep the price stable, and imports are discouraged. Furthermore, the projected "oil gap" fails to consider the development of additional fuel sources, now proceeding full speed ahead Nuclear and solar energy, as well as new methods for higher fuel harvests from existing sources, may make the pipeline obsolete before it is completed.

When the Draft Impact Statement was presented at Washington pipeline hearings, January, 1971, a report issued by the Bureau of Land Management was entered into the *Congressional Record* by Representative Les Aspin of Wisconsin. Its author, Harold Jorgenson, concluded that the Statement's summary assumes "what's good for the oil industry is good for the country." As a result, the Department of the Interior not only failed to consider the full extent of environmental disruption but also neglected alternatives to the pipeline, such as a trans-Canadian route.

The impropriety of the Draft Impact Statement led to a suit filed by the Wilderness Society to halt proceedings pending a complete impact statement which would include adequate safeguards. Trout Unlimited entered the case as *amicus curiae,* presenting its own evidence of potential watershed damage. The injunction was granted, and it took one and a half years for the Secretary of the Interior to complete an adequate impact statement. During that time, at least, Alyeska engineers were able to develop a pipeline design which would minimize environmental disruptions.

The Final Impact Statement, which details potential damage, though not to the satisfaction of conservationists, provides for the mitigation of damages to natives. But the disruption of the Alaskan ecosystem due to construction of the pipeline and certain spills cannot begin to be rectified by any amount of money. The question then comes down to which resource is the more rare and valuable, the oil or the wilderness. Even among the oilmen, there are those who cast their vote for the latter.

At this writing, Secretary Morton has just issued the permit to begin construction. The Wilderness Society, on behalf of other environmentalists, will appeal its case to a higher court in an effort to halt the project until environmental safeguards are a certainty or the pipeline is rerouted along a more suitable course. Trout Unlimited's position, now as before, is that prior to any construction a complete and thorough environmental study must prove that the pipeline will not result in major environmental damage and that all possible alternatives including the trans-Canadian route be thoroughly studied and evaluated.

Experts agree that building the pipeline and preventing environmental destruction are diametrically opposed. Says Tom Brown, whose *Oil on Ice* details the Alaskan situation without the usual polemics, "To get the oil out without altering the land and the quality of the water is beyond man's current technological capabilities." To hope that those capabilities improve during the course of construction is courting irreparable disaster.

Forty percent of America's total supply of fresh water coexists with 10 percent of its wilderness, hardly an impressive percentage. Alaska remains even now, with its litter, sewage problems, and oil spills, the greatest expanse of wilderness left in this country. Preventive conservation alone can save it. If man has learned nothing from the devastation he has wreaked on the rest of his planet, he is indeed writing the last verse of his swan song.

8. organize

CONCERNED INDIVIDUALS ARE the cadre of the environmental militia. Singly they can be very effective. Richard Buck may be credited with saving the North Atlantic salmon, G. M. Brandborg with preserving the Bitterroot. Yet even these two men did not succeed alone. They were responsible for generating the movements, but victory belongs to all those who joined the fight.

Without exception, the same sincere investment of time and effort will count for more if an individual is part of a well-organized group. He would be wise to affiliate straight off with a national organization. Although local organizations can be effective, their scope is limited. National bureaucracies, like those discussed in Chapter 1, are notoriously impervious to local action. A national organization has the clout to succeed. Therefore, find a national conservationist group that has proven its effectiveness. Examine its aims, its organization, and its track record. Then, if it is accomplishing what you want to accomplish, join, not as an onlooker but as an active member.

Through the Natural Resources Council of America, Trout Unlimited has worked with many such conservation groups. The Sierra Club, Wilderness Society, Friends of the Earth, the National Audubon Society, Izaak Walton League, and others have been indispensable allies. Organizationally, however, they differ 180 degrees from TU. Their strong national organization dictates to loosely affiliated local units, in contrast to TU's national dependence on local efforts. Without presuming to imply that there is a single right way, Trout Unlimited has found its structure more suitable for fulfilling its aims: the preservation, protection, and enhancement of the cold-water fishery.

There is nothing mystical or magic about this organization of more than 15,000 fishermen who love their sport enough to fight for it. The organization is simple, and it works. TU begins at the grass roots with 168 chapters reaching from Manchester, New Hampshire, to Seattle, Washington; in addition there are ten councils with regional and national offices to serve them (see the Appendix listings).

The Local TU Chapter

Each chapter is assigned watchdog responsibilities for its specific geographic area. There they are entrusted with fulfilling TU's "preservation, protection, and enhancement" dictum. Methodology, of course, varies from chapter to chapter, running the gamut from teaching local children the art of fishing or conservation to all-out legal battles to halt ill-conceived Federal projects. The variety is due primarily to divergent geography. In the East, the chapters are faced principally with the problems of restoring streams that have been channeled, dammed, or polluted. In the West, TU tackles the Bureau of Reclamation, the Army Corps of Engineers, *et al.* in an effort to prevent environmental destruction.

If the chapter can meet its responsibility within the local sphere, it does so. The yo-yo mailings of the Catskill Chapter, the reclassification drive in at Littleton's Cutthroat Chapter, the Gray's Run project of the Susquehanna Chapter are all examples of fully successful conservation battles waged entirely by local affiliates. Other battles have required intra-agency cooperation. In these cases, the local agency ferreted out the problem and then contacted the state or regional council for support.

The Tocks Island battle began with the Sparta Chapter and later involved the Pennsylvania and New York councils for coordinating aid in pressing for the victory. The mechanics of this structural interdependence are even plainer in a recent skirmish in Colorado.

The Ferdinand-Hayden Chapter, Aspen, makes its headquarters in a Rocky Mountain ski resort through which flows a fine trout river. The chapter guards this river as zealously as a mother grizzly watches her cubs. One day, the chapter president received a call from the local newspaper editor that an asphalt batch plant operating in conjunction with a highway project was dumping effluent into the river. The highway contractor's trucks were being cleaned the same way.

A TU member was dispatched to the scene. Confirming the telephone report, he informed the job foreman that this practice was illegally polluting the stream. An exchange of invectives followed before the foreman concluded with "Get the hell out of here. Now!" Realizing that a judicious step backward often results in many more forward, the TU member returned to the chapter.

Within hours, the chapter leadership conferred with the local game warden, who explained that his hands were tied until there was proof of an actual fish kill, in which case it could take months or even years to repair the damage. If the local unit had not been a part of a larger organization, the unfortunate fact is that the chapter would have been stopped cold. In this case, the chapter president immediately contacted the state council chairman and relayed the pertinent facts.

The council chairman conferred with the head of his water pollution committee to determine the best pressure point, the State Water Pollution Control Commission. He called the Commission, and the next morning an inspector was at the site. By 2 P.M. a local judge had issued a cease-and-desist order, closing the batch plant until operation corrections were made. From the editor's phone call to the halting order, less than twenty-four hours had elapsed. A delay of even eight hours more might have meant the death of the river.

The TU Council

Three or more chapters in a state or region may wish to form a council to coordinate their activities. With two representatives from each of the constituent chapters, the council subdivides into committees to mirror those in the individual chapters to form a chain of communication. Then, if a chapter's dam committee, for example, needs help, its chairman goes directly to the chairman of the council's dam committee for the most effective course of action.

Besides its coordinative function, the council presents a unified front to the state legislature, state agencies, and departments. It also serves as liaison between the local chapters and National Trout Unlimited.

National TU

TU is a volunteer action organization. In order that the chapter's volunteer time may be concentrated on important battles, National TU provides a mailing service whereby each chapter receives the newsletters and announcements of every other chapter to achieve a cross-fertilization of ideas. In addition, a quarterly periodical details

136

chapter and national activities, scientific breakthroughs, and research sponsored by TU and other conservation groups.

As has been stated again and again, facts are the sure-fire weapons of the war. To this end, TU maintains extensive research files. From this armory, the local, state, and national troops ready themselves for battle. The files also enable the national organization to publish national periodicals and produce audiovisual aids used across the country, as was the case with the film *Pass Creek*. The files have provided information necessary for conservationist advertising, like the full-page ad in the *New York Times* and the *Washington Post* taken by the Sierra Club, Wilderness Society, National Audubon Society, and Trout Unlimited urging the protection of Alaska's public lands.

As state and regional TU councils provide a point of contact for state legislatures, agencies, and departments, National TU presents the same kind of unified front to national organizations, including the United States Congress. Besides the organization's nerve center in Denver, TU maintains an office in Washington, D.C., that works on matters emanating from Congress and the many political bureaus and agencies headquartered in that city. This office frequently provides immediate problem-solving by going straight to the top of an offending national agency.

In one case the Colorado Council received a call from one of the state's twelve chapters reporting that a U.S. Forest Service road-building project was conducting a gravel dredging and washing operation in the middle of a mountain stream. When the state council contacted the regional office of the Forest Service, it was told nothing would be done. So the council called the capital office. From there it was a simple matter for the TU representative to track down the right Forest Service bureaucrat and obtain a corrected directive for the Colorado project.

Among National TU's responsibilities is recruitment. To continue the battle, reinforcements are needed. A fisherman, however, is not characteristically a joiner. His sport is a solitary one—but it reaches great tenacity. For this reason, once organized into an effective action group, no one rivals a fisherman in dedication and resolve. Apathy remains the greatest single threat to natural resources, an enemy far more dangerous than the Corps or BuRec or any of the others. As surely as the fisherman's participation in the war means victory, his hesitancy means defeat. His sport depends on his decision. So does his future.

How to Form a Trout Unlimited Chapter

The seed of a TU chapter usually begins with a small group of TU members who are unhappy with the fisheries in their area. (The national headquarters in Denver will provide a listing of members in any particular area.) They then hold several informal meetings to draw up their organization plan and compose a list of potential members. This list should be as long as possible, including every serious fisherman in the area, sportscasters and outdoor editors, and local and state conservation officials. Once a copy of this list is forwarded to National TU, all mailings will be handled free of charge.

At the same time, the potential chapter should make key newspaper, radio, and television contacts. Whenever possible these contacts should be made in person to further cooperation. Media lent invaluable support in CASE's fight for the North Atlantic salmon, in the Cutthroat Chapter's battle to prevent channeling of the South Platte, and in the Aspen Chapter's press for a new sewage treatment plant. The support of allies in the news media ought to be assured from a chapter's beginning.

The next step is setting the date of the official chapter formation. Potential members and the news media should be contacted at least two weeks in advance; a second notice is advisable. Experience recommends presenting both the media and the potential membership with a portfolio about Trout Unlimited and its program. Such material will be provided by the national headquarters.

To prepare for the formation meeting, the nucleus of the organization should arrange for a TU official, either a national officer or a director of another chapter or council, to attend the meeting. They should also plan a slate of officers: president, vice-president, and secretary-treasurer. If this should prove difficult, the attendant TU official may appoint officers to serve until elections are held.

At the formation meeting, the TU official will explain the organization and its principles and secure an affirmative motion that those attending wish to form a chapter. Then the new chapter president will conduct the naming of the chapter and outline a proposed program of action. Immediate commitment to a project is critically important to the launching of a new chapter, because it encourages the genuine participation of the new members.

Each chapter must draw up its own set of bylaws. As an autonomous unit, it is free to determine its own structural mechanics so long as it operates to carry out the objectives of the national organization. National Headquarters will provide sample bylaws if so requested by the new chapter.

When the bylaws have been approved by the membership, a copy must be sent to the Board of Directors at the national headquarters with the request for chapter certification. The letter should include the chapter name, a copy of the minutes of the organizational meeting, the names, addresses, and brief biographies of all chapter officers and directors, and any available publicity of the meeting. Then to work: "Take action" is the only demand made by National TU.

There is no question that conservationists are successful and becoming more so all the time. The days of wholesale destruction are over, but only continued vigilance will keep it that way. Battles have been waged and won from one coast to the other. Environmentalists have preserved wild, rushing rivers in the Northwest, protected clear and cold streams in the South, and enhanced the fisheries of the East. Their victories are won for all; each makes our collective future more certain.

By now, "What can I do?" has surely been answered. What remains is to do it!

appendix

Trout Unlimited's National Office,
Councils, and Chapters

NATIONAL OFFICE: TROUT UNLIMITED
4260 East Evans Avenue
Denver, Colorado   80222

STATE COUNCILS: COLORADO COUNCIL
26 Martin Lane
Englewood, Colorado   80110

MICHIGAN COUNCIL
700 Fisher Building
Detroit, Michigan   48202

MONTANA COUNCIL
P.O. Box 1285
Livingston, Montana   59047

NEW JERSEY COUNCIL
2200 North Central Road
Fort Lee, New Jersey   07024

NEW YORK STATE COUNCIL
P.O. Box 162
Lake Katrine, New York   12449

NORTH CAROLINA COUNCIL
363C South By Pass
Lenoir, North Carolina   28645

NORTHWEST STEELHEADERS COUNCIL
P.O. Box 2841
Portland, Oregon   97408
(This council represents
Oregon, Washington, Idaho.)

PENNSYLVANIA COUNCIL
795 East Pike
Indiana, Pennsylvania   15701

UTAH COUNCIL
3277 Tyler Avenue
Ogden, Utah   84403

WISCONSIN COUNCIL
1311 Farwell Drive
Madison, Wisconsin   53704

LOCAL CHAPTERS:

Alabama   Shades Valley Chapter, Birmingham

Alaska   Rainbow Chapter, Anchorage

California   Burney/Mount Lassen Chapter, Burney
San Diego County Chapter, Encinitas
San Francisco Bay Area Chapter, San Francisco
Santa Clara Valley Chapter, Santa Clara
Southern California Chapter, Beverly Hills

Colorado   Boulder Flycasters Chapter, Boulder
Cutthroat Chapter, Littleton
Eagle Valley Chapter, Vail

Ferdinand-Hayden Chapter, Aspen
Greeley Chapter, Greeley
Gunnison County Chapter, Gunnison
Lee Wulff Chapter, Northglenn
Poudre-Big Thompson Chapter, Fort Collins
South Platte Chapter, Lakewood
Swandyke Chapter, Breckenridge
Ute Chapter, Colorado Springs
Wild Trout Chapter, Aurora

District of Columbia National Capital Chapter, Washington

Georgia Chattahoochee Chapter, Atlanta

Idaho Idaho Panhandle Chapter, Priest River
Kendrick-Juliaetta Chapter, Moscow
Orofino Chapter, Orofino
Treasure Valley Chapter, Boise
Upper Snake River Chapter, Idaho Falls

Illinois Greater Chicago Chapter, Arlington Heights

Maine Sunkhaze Stream Chapter, Oldtown

Maryland Maryland Chapter, Baltimore

Massachusetts Massachusetts Chapter, Boston
Three Rivers Chapter, Framingham
Worcester County Chapter, Worcestor

Michigan Ann Arbor Chapter, Ann Arbor
Corey-Eldredge Chapter, Big Rapids
Flint Chapter, Flint
George W. Mason Chapter, Grayling
Grand Traverse Chapter, Traverse City
Hazen Miller Chapter, Petoskey
Jackson Chapter, Jackson
Kalamazoo Valley Chapter, Kalamazoo
Lansing Chapter, Lansing
Paul H. Young Chapter, Bloomfield Hills
West Michigan Chapter, Grand Rapids
William B. Mershon Chapter, Saginaw

Minnesota Minnesota Chapter, Minneapolis

Montana	Beartooth Chapter, Billings
	Big Spring Creek Chapter, Lewistown
	Flathead Chapter, St. Ignatius
	Great Falls Chapter, Great Falls
	Madison-Gallatin Chapter, Bozeman
	Missouri River Chapter, Helena
	West Slope Chapter, Missoula
	Yellowstone River Chapter, Livingston
Nebraska	Western Nebraska Chapter, Ogallala
Nevada	Nevada Chapter, Reno
New Hampshire	Manchester Chapter, Manchester
	New Hampshire Chapter, Peterborough
	Winnepesaukie Chapter, Laconia
New Jersey	Central Jersey Chapter, North Brunswick
	East Jersey Chapter, Fort Lee
	North Jersey Chapter, Sparta
New Mexico	Rio Grande Chapter, Albuquerque
	Truchas Chapter, Santa Fe
New York	Al Hazzard Chapter, Binghamton
	Catskill Mountain Chapter, Kingston
	Chautauqua Chapter, Jamestown
	Clear Water Chapter, Albany
	Croton Watershed Chapter, Brewster
	Iroquois Chapter, Syracuse
	Long Island Chapter, Syosset
	Mohawk Valley Chapter, Utica
	Ray Bergman Chapter, Congers
	Robert O. Willsey Chapter, Ithaca
	Seth Green Chapter, Rochester
	Western New York Chapter, Buffalo
North Carolina	Blue Ridge Chapter, Winston-Salem
	Daniel Boone Chapter, Boone
	Land of Sky Chapter, Asheville
	Northwest North Carolina Chapter, Morganton
	Piedmont Chapter, Charlotte
	Pisgah Chapter, Brevard
	Tuckasegee Chapter, Bryson City

Ohio	Johnny Appleseed Chapter, Shelby
	Northwest Ohio Chapter, Toledo
	Western Reserve Chapter, Twinsburg
Oregon	Albany Chapter, Shedd
	Angler's Club of Portland, Portland
	Beaverton Chapter, Beaverton
	Crater Lake Chapter, Central Point
	Deaf Chapter, Portland
	Deschutes Chapter, Bend
	Elgin Chapter, Elgin
	Eugene Chapter, Eugene
	Hillsboro Chapter, Hillsboro
	Island City Chapter, La Grande
	La Grande Chapter, La Grande
	Madras Chapter, Madras
	Mid-Willamette Valley Chapter, Salem
	Milwaukie Chapter, Milwaukie
	Mount Hood Chapter, Wemme
	North Portland Chapter, Portland
	Oregon City Chapter, Oregon City
	Portland Chapter, Portland
	Roseburg Chapter, Sutherlin
	Sandy River Chapter, Troutdale
	South Umpqua Chapter, Tiller
	Southwest Oregon Chapter, Coos Bay
	Tigard Chapter, Tigard
	Tillamook Chapter, Tillamook
	Union Chapter, Union
Pennsylvania	Allegheny Mountain Chapter, Punxsutawney
	Cross Fork Chapter, Cross Fork
	Cumberland Valley Chapter, Carlisle
	Donegal Chapter, Mount Joy
	Eastern Pennsylvania Chapter, Philadelphia
	Evergreen Chapter, Indiana
	Freestone Chapter, Berwick
	Monocacy Chapter, Allentown
	Mountain Laurel Chapter, Johnstown
	Northwest Pennsylvania Chapter, Waterford
	Penns Creek Chapter, Lewistown

144

	Penn's Woods West Chapter, Pittsburgh
	Raymond B. Winter Chapter, Mifflinburg
	South Central Pennsylvania Chapter, Altoona
	Susquehanna Chapter, Williamsport
	Tri County Chapter, Saxton
South Carolina	South Carolina Chapter, Greenville
Tennessee	Appalachian Chapter, Chattanooga
	Cherokee Chapter, Athens
	Great Smokey Mountain Chapter, Knoxville
Texas	Dallas Chapter, Dallas
	Guadalupe Chapter, Houston
Utah	Logan River Chapter, Logan
	Ogden River Chapter, Ogden
	Provo River Chapter, Provo
	Salt Lake Chapter, Salt Lake City
Vermont	Battenkill Chapter, Manchester
	Central Vermont Chapter, Winooski
Virginia	Southwestern Virginia Chapter, Roanoke
Washington	Al Pritchard Chapter, Kelso
	Bellevue Chapter, Bellevue
	Bremerton Chapter, Bremerton
	Elliot Bay Chapter, Renton
	Everett Chapter, Everett
	Gray Harbor Chapter, Aberdeen
	Inland Empire Chapter, Spokane
	North Seattle Chapter, Seattle
	Peninsula Chapter, Port Angeles
	Seattle Chapter, Seattle
	Seattle Businessmen's Luncheon Chapter, Seattle
	Sno King Chapter, Lynnwood
	South King County Chapter, Federal Way
	Tacoma Chapter, Tacoma
	Three Rivers Chapter, Kennewick
	Upper Columbia Chapter, Wenatchee
	Vancouver Chapter, Vancouver
	Washougal River Chapter, Camas
	Yakima Chapter, Yakima

West Virginia	Kanawha Valley Chapter, Charleston
	Mountaineer Chapter, Clarksburg
Wisconsin	Central Wisconsin Chapter, Wautoma
	Green Bay Chapter, Green Bay
	Kiap-Tu-Wish Chapter, Hudson
	Southeast Wisconsin Chapter, Milwaukee
	Southern Wisconsin Chapter, Madison
	Wolf River Chapter, White Lake
Wyoming	Jackson Hole Fly Fisherman Chapter, Jackson
	Snowy Range Chapter, Laramie
	Upper Green River Chapter, Pinedale